Thérèse of Lisieux

Thérèse of
Lisieux

MONICA FURLONG

DARTON · LONGMAN + TODD

First published in Great Britain in 1987 by
Virago Press Limited

This edition published in 2001 by
Darton, Longman and Todd Ltd
1 Spencer Court
140–142 Wandsworth High Street
London SW18 4JJ

Reprinted 2001

© 1987 and 2001 Monica Furlong

ISBN 0-232-52418-1

A catalogue record for this book is available from the British
Library

Printed and bound in Great Britain by
Page Bros, Norwich, Norfolk

CONTENTS

Chronology   vii

Introduction   1

Chapter 1
For Ever and Ever   11

Chapter 2
The Little Queen   24

Chapter 3
Born for Greatness   38

Chapter 4
A Drop Lost in the Ocean   51

Chapter 5
A Toy of No Value   64

Chapter 6
The Little Bride   74

Chapter 7
The Little Way   92

Chapter 8
A Very Little Saint   106

Chapter 9
The Shower of Roses   121

Conclusion   129

Bibliography   136

Notes   138

Index   141

CHRONOLOGY

1873	*2 January:* birth of Marie-Françoise-Thérèse Martin, the ninth and last child of Louis and Zélie Martin, at 36 rue Saint-Blaise, Alençon, Normandy. *4 January:* baptised, with her sister Marie as godmother. *March:* goes to live with a 'wet nurse' – Rose Taillé, at Semallé.
1874	*April:* returns to live with her family.
1875	Thinks that she will be a nun when she grows up.
1877	*28 August:* death of Thérèse's mother, Zélie. Thérèse's choice of Pauline as her substitute-mother, 'ma petite mère'. *November:* the Martin family go to live at Lisieux.
1879	First confession.
1881	Begins going to school at the Benedictine Abbey.
1882	Pauline enters the Lisieux Carmel.
1882–1883	*December–May:* Thérèse suffers from acute nervous illness.
1883	*13 May:* Thérèse's illness is cured by a vision of the Virgin.
1884	*8 May:* First Communion. *14 June:* Confirmation.
1886	Thérèse leaves school, studies privately with Mme Papinau. *25 December:* has the religious experience she described as 'conversion'.
1887	*March:* Louis Martin suffers his first stroke. *May:* Louis gives Thérèse permission to enter Carmel. *July:* Thérèse prays for the murderer Pranzini. *October:* Thérèse and Louis visit the Bishop of

Bayeux in an attempt to win his approval for her entering Carmel at fifteen. *November:* Thérèse, Céline and Louis take a European tour. *20 November:* an audience with the Pope in which Thérèse begs him to let her enter Carmel.

1888   *9 April:* Thérèse enters Carmel as a postulant.

1889   *10 January:* Thérèse takes the habit at Carmel, and becomes a novice.

1890   *8 September:* Thérèse is 'professed' – takes her life vows. *24 September:* Thérèse 'takes the veil' – starts wearing the black veil of the professed nun instead of the white one of the novice, and is henceforth known as 'Soeur Thérèse de l'Enfant Jésus et de la Sainte Face'.

1891   *December:* influenza epidemic.

1893   Thérèse becomes assistant novice mistress.

1894   Thérèse writes the play *'Jeanne d'Arc'* and acts the title role. Has her throat cauterised for soreness and hoarseness. Death of Louis Martin. Ordered by Pauline – Mother Agnes – to write memories of her childhood.

1895   Becomes the 'spiritual sister' of a missionary and starts praying for him and corresponding with him.

1896   *January:* Thérèse gives the finished manuscript to Pauline. *April:* Thérèse suffers the first haemorrhage from her lungs. Finishes second part of her autobiography.

1897   *April:* becomes very ill. Is permitted a regime of rest, treatment and a slightly improved diet. *June:* Thérèse writes the third part of her autobiography. *30 July:* Extreme Unction given. *19 August:* Last Communion. *30 September:* death of Thérèse.

1898   *September:* 2000 copies of *Histoire d'une Ame* (the Story of a Soul) published.

1899   *October:* a second edition – 4000 copies – of

Thérèse's autobiography published.

1906–1923   Formal proceedings towards Thérèse's canonisation take place.

1923   *April:* beatification of Thérèse.

1925   *May:*canonisation of St Thérèse at St Peter's, Rome.

INTRODUCTION

Thérèse of Lisieux, sweet, childlike, obedient, tragic, has been until recent times a cherished icon of Catholic womanhood. Although close in time to our own period – she died shortly before the turn of the century and her sister Céline survived until 1959 – she has been cast in one of the favourite moulds of traditional female sanctity, the mould of virginity, of suffering, of drastic self-abnegation. Vita Sackville-West, even in the first flush of Christian discovery, had another complaint about Thérèse. She accused her of what the French call *niaiserie*, sugariness.

It is a little embarrassing, therefore, to admit that I have been fascinated by Thérèse of Lisieux for years, ever since reading Ronald Knox's translation of her autobiography *Autobiography of a Saint* more than twenty years ago. Partly this was because her vivacious account of life in the Martin family touched upon something in my own experience – like her I was the youngest member of the family, was close to my father and had a fractured experience of my mother. More even than this, I was captivated by her account of her adolescent passion for God. Like many girls, I was haunted by God in my teens, but I sensed that this was an embarrassing, even slightly improper, state of feeling in twentieth-century England. Thérèse not only demonstrates the passion for God with great thoroughness, she also shows the devastating effect that it had on her life, cutting her off from ordinary human contact at the age of fifteen, to die at twenty-four. What health or pathology we are bound to ask, or what mixture of the two, pushed her into this obsession with ultimate relationship?

As we begin to ask these questions we find ourselves also asking hard questions of the Christian religion, of its interpretations of its basic doctrines, of its attitudes to women and the way these shaped European culture and affected women like Thérèse. One of the most interesting things about Thérèse's story is seeing the way Christian attitudes, Jansenist Catholic attitudes in her case, impinged upon a very intelligent, passionate and sensual little girl.

Christianity had inherited many of its attitudes to women from Judaism, a religion in which women exercised little or no power outside the family, and were explicitly regarded as inferior to men. Although Jesus clearly treated women with respect, even partiality, Christian attitudes, like those of Judaism, were shaped by the myth of Adam and Eve, in which woman was seen as the dangerous temptress who, unless firmly controlled, would drag man with her into destruction. Although it seems as if women played some part in the leadership of the early Church, teaching, caring for the poor, offering hospitality in their homes so that Christian rites could be enacted there, within a generation or two of Jesus' death they had been relegated to the silent role advocated by St Paul.

Other forces affected the role of women. The Middle East in the first century abounded in fertility cults in which women, as priestesses, enjoyed privileged status. In its need to find a separate identity, to be seen as distinct from a paganism which may have given a central importance to sexuality and sensuality, the young Church followed a different pattern and rejected women as potential leaders. Although many women died as martyrs, their voice, and therefore much of their formative influence on Christianity, was lost.

Greek thought also profoundly influenced the young Church. Mind or spirit were seen as distinctly separate from body, a dualistic concept very different from Judaistic ideas.

In the third century Manes developed the ideas which became known as Manicheism, a way of seeing the world as a total conflict between good and evil – another form of dualism. The religious believer, by practising all kinds of austerities, in particular by rejecting sexuality, sided with the forces of good. The Christian church rejected the ideas of Manes as heretical, but it never lost the idea of a dramatic split at the heart of experience, one which would resurface in Christian thought again and again. The split, and the agony it produced, seemed to appeal more to the Christian imagination than a sense of the unity of the world, of God and all the creatures within the world, of spirit and matter. Fantasies of conflict and punishment seemed to recur more often than fantasies of unity and bliss, although, as in all religions, mystics did speak of transcending the dualisms and achieving ecstasy.

On the whole, though, dualism remained dominant, despite a belief in a God who became human, of spirit becoming incarnated in flesh, and of the consequent sacramental understanding of a world in which matter showed forth the divine. In spite of the central Christian rite in which the body of God was eaten (literally or symbolically according to different schools of thought) Christianity retained an obstinately 'spiritual' or 'disembodied' attitude, preferring saints who had not been 'tainted' by sexual experience, priests (within Catholicism) who eschewed marriage, and followers who, often enough, showed a harsh and rigorous attitude to the body.

Sexuality, the outcome of attraction to creatures (matter), somehow turned into the enemy of the God who had invented it. Woman, the most attractive of the creatures, aroused the strongest sexual feelings and was therefore, if not the enemy herself, at least implicated on the wrong side of the struggle between good and evil. The writings of the Fathers saw woman as dangerous, a source of temptation. Saint Augustine did not believe that she was made in the image of God, a personal disaster she could only redeem by subordinating herself to a husband who *was* made in the image of God. (Later St Thomas Aquinas was to suggest that woman was a sort of botched male.) She must be dominated, supervised, by men so that her mischief could not wreak havoc.

By the Middle Ages celibacy had become the noblest option for men who loved God, an option that allowed, positively encouraged, them to avoid women as much as possible. Even the saintly Francis, who loved birds and animals and embraced lepers, advised his disciples, according to his biographer Bonaventure, never to so much as look a woman in the face if they could help it. Woman, in person, had somehow become 'the body', the contaminated matter against which the would-be spiritual person had to strive.

Quite why women should be drawn to a religion that treated them so woundingly is an interesting question. Perhaps on the deepest level they understood Christianity better than it officially understood itself, and were nourished and comforted by it as the black slaves of America would come to be comforted by it in a society that had no human place for them at all. Forbidden all leadership, not permitted to raise their voices in public, to perform rites, to preach or teach, women still clung to the religion which spoke of love, sharing and compassion, faithful in prayer, religious devotions, and acts of charity.

One of the ambiguities of their situation was the passionate devotion accorded to the Virgin Mary. Men who had separated themselves from any contact with flesh and blood women, or who at least thought it desirable to do so, nevertheless gave tremendous honour to the Mother of Christ. Undoubtedly some sense of self-worth and esteem, deriving from Mary, was felt by Christian women, though as an ideal for women she was seriously wanting. As celibate as the priests who were devoted to her, able, as no other woman was able, to conceive without the 'contamination' of sexuality, she offered a kind of model that could only very approximately be copied. Her self-abnegation, in accepting the will of God, and her suffering, in seeing her son die, were enjoined upon women as their religious role.

One way to follow her example was for women to embark upon motherhood with as little sexuality as was practically possible. Another way, though it involved sacrificing both sexuality and the opportunity to bear children, was by becoming a celibate in a religious community – a nun. Religious communities for women were ultimately governed by men – their abbesses controlled by monks, priests and bishops. The life, in theory, and very often in fact, was a penitential one, intended both to redeem the sin of Eve and the sinfulness of the world.

Despite considerable restrictions, however, convents often offered women opportunities that were not otherwise available to them – education, freedom not to marry, or not to be controlled by the family, freedom from uncontrolled child-bearing, freedom from the dangers of licentious societies with an exploitative attitude to women, the chance of exercising limited leadership (some of the medieval abbesses were very powerful, usually because of aristocratic connections), the pleasure of living with congenial women and leading a life of order, prayer, and maybe intellectual and aesthetic satisfaction.

Alongside the positive aspects of the life, however, and along-side the sacrifice of sexuality and motherhood, there was, in many convents, physical discomfort and hunger, brief periods of sleep, humiliations of various kinds and flagellation. The body was punished to exalt the spirit, and in the effort to achieve 'detachment from creatures' the simplest appetites and pleasures were denied. Inevitably, it seems to us now, many women who lived such lives succumbed to illness and early death.

It is this history that we need to have in mind when we consider Thérèse. Brought up in a household run rather like a convent, she inherited a religion that had shown an attitude of little more than toleration towards women for hundreds of years. (During the periods of the persecution of witches even toleration had broken down.) A secret ambition of Thérèse's, secret because it was forbidden to women, was to be a priest. Of course, she knew that there was no question of it, since there was no such thing as a woman priest in Catholicism, but the longing lodged in her mind, and as she lay dying she confided to her sister that she was glad she would be dead before the age at which young men were admitted to the priesthood, that she felt this was a great kindness on God's part to save her from dis-appointment.

Priesthood apart, for her, as for most young women of the middle class in nineteenth-century France, the choice was between marriage and the convent, that is to say between uncontrolled childbearing within a relationship which might, or might not, be of the girl's own choosing, or a life without sexual expression. Independence was scarcely a possible choice.

Thérèse had had the chance to observe the first of these alternatives. Her mother, Zélie Martin, had borne nine children within thirteen years, nearly all of them suffering a very sickly infancy. Four of them died within the first few years of life. In the later years of her childbearing Mme Martin was afflicted with breast cancer, and in addition to the exhaustion of her illness, and her grief at the loss of her children, she had the added stress of running her lace-making business.

Thérèse's early childhood was spent in a small Norman town, Alençon, whose claim to fame was its lace-making industry. After Zélie died the Martin family exchanged Alençon for another small town, Lisieux. The Martins lived the life of provincial bourgeois Catholicism.

It was a Catholicism still in reaction to the Age of Enlightenment and to Voltaire's attacks upon the Church. Normandy, and more particularly Lisieux, was the scene of an enormous struggle between Catholics, usually royalist and anti-semitic (like Thérèse's uncle Isidore), and republicans, usually agnostic or atheistic and profoundly anticlerical. Two weekly newspapers, on different sides of the conflict, *le Normand* and *le Lexovien*, continually exacerbated it. This bitter fight was the background to Thérèse's religious upbringing.

To their clericalism and sense of belonging to a religion under siege the Martins brought a peculiar rigour of their own, a Jansenist note that was by no means common to all Catholics. Jansenism, deriving from the seventeenth-century theologian Cornelius Jansen, propagated by his friend and disciple Saint-Cyran, and the convent of Port-Royal, offered an extraordinarily pessimistic interpretation of the Christian religion. Like Calvinism, with which it had many parallels, it believed grace to be irresistible, with the deterministic consequence that, as in the doctrines of predestination, one was set for salvation or damnation in spite of oneself. The longing to find oneself in the camp of the saved led to a moral rigorism, a tendency to despise the folly and vanity of this world, and to long for death and the joys of the hereafter. There was a profound suspicion of the life of the senses, and a method of continual self-examination which was meant to root out faults and cultivate virtues. What it cultivated less intentionally were morbid scruples, depression and a fear of damnation.

The world into which Thérèse emerged, therefore, was defensively Catholic, morbidly concerned with virtue, and fascinated by death. The life of her family was concentrated upon the Church, with a limited interest in matters outside religion, such as art or letters. There was warmth and love both within the immediate family circle and within the extended family of aunts and cousins, and there was, presumably, a sense of intimacy in the small town atmosphere of Lisieux, though this does not especially feature either in family letters or in Thérèse's writing. In practice this life may have been claustrophobic, but no one who grew up within it could believe themselves a matter of indifference to others – on the contrary every detail of life and of relationship was a matter of the utmost interest and the continual subject of reflection and speculation in family letters. Despite all her responsibilities Zélie Martin wrote letters almost daily to her brother and sister-in-law discussing her children, her business, and her health.

It is partly because there is such an immensity of detail known about the life of Thérèse and the life of her family that she is so interesting. Both she and her mother are natural writers and have a gift for fixing upon small, compelling details that bring an alien world vividly alive for us. Both of them have a taste for trivia (it is no accident that Thérèse's understanding of spirituality – the Little Way, as she called it – is a form of spirituality concerned with apparently trivial events and details) and we learn to understand Thérèse through minutiae. I have used many of these details to try to show the reader the saint and her life. They are not unlike a photographic record which can take us in an instant into a world very different from our own.

As it happens the life of Thérèse was contemporaneous with the growing popularity of photography, and Thérèse's sister

Céline loved to use a camera. So that alongside the descriptive gifts of the Martin family we have photographs of the saint as a tiny girl, as an eager seven-year-old wearing earrings, as a fifteen-year-old who had put her hair up in an attempt to look grown-up to impress the bishop, and throughout her brief years in the convent.

I think that it is rare to know as much about any dead person as we know about Thérèse; of some periods of her life we know not only what happened but exactly what she was feeling. It is an intimate knowledge that, usually, we have only of characters in a novel, and at times I find myself thinking of Thérèse as a character in a novel, as someone with whom I have enjoyed a literary intimacy. At one point in the book, the part where she enters Carmel, so confident was I of her thoughts and emotions that I have described the event with the innerness of a novelist, a slightly dangerous habit in a biographer but one which felt appropriate here since the innerness was so well documented.

Quite apart from the intrinsic interest of Thérèse's life – the life of a nineteenth-century French girl, the life of an enclosed nun in the Carmelite order – there is the fact that she is known as a saint. St Paul, and the earliest Christian writers, spoke of 'saints' rather than 'a saint' meaning the community of the faithful, God's holy people, a usage which appeared again among the Calvinist communities of the seventeenth century, who thought of the saints as, collectively, 'the elect'.

The lives of the martyrs from the first century onward were of a quality of such extraordinary heroism that a special term seemed to be needed and gradually the word 'saint' began to be applied to such individuals. Their bodily remains, together with their belongings, began to be collected and preserved as items containing some special spiritual quality, and their names became favourite names to give to Christian children in baptism. Already by AD 220 Tertullian, the Church Father, was protesting against the superstition and excess which surrounded the cult of saints.

The first saints were simply recognised and admired by local churches or by local bishops. Sometimes their fame would spread outside their own neighbourhood or country and they would come to be revered in places far away. Such saints were created as a result of popular enthusiasm and taste, a taste which the bishops then endorsed.

During the tenth century in the western church this informal method began to change and henceforward the Pope reserved the right to make saints. From 1634 a very formal method was established, what was and is called canonisation, one that involved a number of elaborate processes – the subject's writings and life had to be meticulously examined, and evidence was taken from relatives, friends and others. It was by this method that Thérèse of Lisieux was made a saint in 1925.

Saints were not, so far as the Church was concerned (the popular belief was different), people who led perfect lives, or who were without faults and failings. 'The saint', says the Oxford Dictionary of Saints, 'is the man or woman who gives himself, herself, to God heroically.' By this standard Thérèse, as we shall see, richly deserved her title.

What is sometimes difficult for a twenty-first-century reader is a sense that motives which once seemed above suspicion – self-denial, bodily mortification, a life lived 'for others' – may contain hidden gratifications, covert claims for glory and power, masochistic solutions to intolerable situations, which for us destroy the sense of wonder. Whether we like it or not – and there is, in most of us, a tendency to enjoy making heroic projections – we find ourselves becoming critical about sanctity, spoiling the idealised picture with psychological questions which detract from the sense of perfection and awestruck admiration once accorded to saints. We note their childhood difficulties, their neurosis, their inability to adapt to normal adult life, their illusions and defences. It is a kind of reductionism which, at first sight, seems to leave us poorer, bereft of the example of those who once seemed to show us how life should be lived.

At first sight, but not at second perhaps. In many ways the women and men who have been called saints become more, not less, remarkable and lovable, when we see their frailty more clearly. We begin to see that their courage and heroism lay in their exploration of the human condition, that their originality resided in knowing the extremes of mind and spirit, as Columbus's lay in exploring the world geographically. Like artists they were able to do this not in spite of the wounding of their psyche but because of it, as neurosis opened them to realms that 'the normal' would never dream of entering. To yearn to know, or love God, as the saint yearned for it, was to want to know the geography of the spirit, to understand what it was to be a human being, but also to know more beside, to set humanity within a larger landscape of meaning.

It was such a landscape that Thérèse, despite hysteria and depression, or because of it, was prepared to explore, despite the low esteem in which she, as a woman, was held in the Church, or because of it. It was a desperate voyage, one so severe that, possibly, she died of its effects. Personally I love her in her pain and conflict in a way that I could never have loved the sugary little saint that so many biographies have depicted. I do not believe that it is true, as so many of her male biographers have suggested, that she was particularly gentle or obedient. Rather she was one who, whatever the obstructions, struggled from her earliest days to make sense of life, and who was prepared to pay any price in order to do so. This is an account of the struggle and the price.

Chapter One

FOR EVER AND EVER

On Monday 9 April 1888, Thérèse set off with her sisters Léonie and Céline and her father to walk to Carmel, the convent she was about to enter. The walk, first downhill from the steep little hill where they lived in a house called Les Buissonets, then uphill, took about twenty minutes. She took Papa's arm – he had tired easily since the stroke a year ago. Once when he saw tears in her eyes he said 'Steady, my little queen' but he was much more tearful than she was.

It was a relief that she had actually set off at last, and the big adventure for which she had planned for so long had begun to happen. She had been so scared that something would prevent it. The last few days had been very difficult. She had to say goodbye to Les Buissonets, which she would never see again. She had visited all her favourite spots, the shrubbery in which she and Céline had played hide and seek, the tower where Papa liked to think his thoughts, the places in the garden where she had built little altars, the room where Pauline had taught her, the alley outside the garden where she had bowled her hoop, the bedroom where once, in delirium, she had seen a vision of the Blessed Virgin, the place where she had told her distraught Papa that she wished to enter Carmel like her two older sisters.

'Never again' – the words had a romantic appeal for her, as she played for the last time with her dog Tom (she felt guilty that she could not explain the situation to him), wandered in and out of the kitchen where she and various maids had played and chatted, chose the few simple possessions she was going to take with her into the convent, objects which the novice mistress might well take away from her.

The last days had been a torment of excitement, with Thérèse longing to start her new life, and then catching Papa's tearful glance resting upon her. Always given to easy tears, as well as to irritable tempers, lately he had got much worse.

On her last day at Les Buissonets the Martins had gone as usual to Sunday Mass at the cathedral of St Pierre and she had made her goodbyes to the chapel where she had prayed so often. That evening her uncle Isidore Guérin and Aunt Céline had come for a farewell meal with her cousins Jeanne and Marie. Victoire had cooked a special dinner, though she knew better than anybody that Thérèse was never very interested in eating. Thérèse looked pretty and Uncle Isidore was unusually complimentary. He proposed a toast to her, though he had strongly disapproved of her entering the convent at fifteen and it had taken all her determination to get her own way. Papa scarcely spoke a word.

When she and her cousin Marie were alone together for a few moments Marie begged her pardon for all the unkind things she had ever done to her. Thérèse could not remember any unkind things Marie had ever done to her, but something in her questions made her think that, unlike Jeanne who was engaged to be married, Marie had secret dreams about the convent herself.

Poor Léonie, despite her own failure to become a nun, was very loving and thoughtful towards Thérèse as always, but her suggestions and little gifts were never quite right, somehow. She always wanted to talk just when Thérèse was getting into something really interesting with Céline, and she never understood the jokes they had together.

Thérèse and Céline had one last night of sharing a room. Thérèse had shared all her dreams of the convent with Céline, as well as her plots to get herself accepted under age. Now that they had achieved what they had worked for, both were so excited it was hard to sleep. The thought of separation was only bearable as a temporary measure.

'Remember,' she had said to Céline, 'one day you must belong to the Carmel too.'

'What about Papa?' Céline had asked.

'Léonie could look after him. She doesn't seem to have a vocation like the rest of us.'

Léonie was the middle one of the five sisters. The two oldest were Marie and Pauline and they were already in Carmel. Léonie had tried her vocation with the Poor Clares and then with the Visitation nuns and had been sent home ignominiously from both convents. She had always been a problem, since she was a tiny child. Their mother had despaired of her. Plain, awkward, obstinate, the odd one out of the Martin sisters, she never seemed happy anywhere.

Thérèse slept little. She was up early, dressed in a simple dress that befitted her new life. Soon she would wear the plain brown dress of a postulant. How she longed for her Clothing, when she would put on the proper habit of a Carmelite nun. It was a relief to be ready to go. At any moment now she would be gone from Les Buissonets for ever.

The road to Carmel followed a route she had often taken on walks with Papa. It was with him that she had first entered the big church there with its grille behind which the nuns sang. When she had been a tiny girl, Papa, on their afternoon walks, had liked to enter churches where the Blessed Sacrament – the consecrated bread and wine – was kept behind its little curtain. There, in the presence of Jesus, he would pray intently. When they left the Carmel church he had explained to her about the nuns and how they devoted their lives to God in a very special way. She liked the pretty front garden of the convent with its white statue of the Virgin, and the pillars and curlicues which made the church look very grand.

When Thérèse was eight her favourite sister Pauline had entered Carmel. Pauline had been the most important person in her life then – ever since her mother had died – and she was very upset at Pauline's going. She had begged the Prioress to let her become a Carmelite at once so that she could stay with her sister. The nuns had laughed at her, and petted her, and let her join her sister sometimes inside the grille, but her sister had gone and that was all there was to it. It had upset her terribly. Later her sister Marie had entered. Now it was her turn. She was much more enthusiastic about it than Marie who had gone in mainly because her confessor told her to. Thérèse could not imagine how you could be so lukewarm about it.

The procession arrived and the whole family was present at Mass and Communion at the Carmelite church. The grille door stood open waiting for her to join the community. She could hear quite loud sniffs and sobs coming from her female relations and specially from Papa. Even Uncle Isidore looked a little moist around the eyes. She was the only dry-eyed one there. What she felt was excitement, her heart beating so fast she felt ready to faint. Soon she would get the signal to move to the convent door and she was so overjoyed it was almost unbearable. She usually did get what she wanted, she noticed, as if God intended it.

One by one her relatives kissed her and then she knelt for a blessing from her father. It was like Papa that he instantly knelt down too, saying 'O little queen!', as he blessed her. She thought the angels would be pleased to see an old man give up his daughter, and the daughter herself give up her freedom. But the poor King of France and Navarre! (The King and Queen of France and Navarre were the pet names the two of them had for each other.) He would miss his favourite daughter.

At last the painful goodbyes came to an end, she passed through the door of the grille where Pauline, Sister Agnes as she was called now, and Marie, Sister Marie of the Sacred Heart, were the first to embrace her. To be held in Pauline's arms and kissed made her feel that she had only left one home to return to another. Then the Prioress, Mother Marie de Gonzague, a dark, fine-looking woman in her fifties, embraced her. She was, Thérèse knew, of noble family, and perhaps this gave her her unusual self-confidence and dignity. No wonder she was constantly re-elected as Superior.

The Novice Mistress, Sister Marie of the Angels, the other aristocrat of this little community, also embraced her. She had a warm, kindly face. Then all the other Sisters hugged her, some rather distantly, others affectionately, and smiled at her – they made her feel they were really glad she was there. She was not so certain of Canon Delatroette, who had made some remark about her to Mother Marie which she did not quite catch but she could tell was sarcastic. He had done everything he could to prevent her being received at such a young age, and now she knew that he hoped she would fail. Probably he thought she was a silly little girl with a crush on the religious life; he did not know how deeply she loved God, how she would do anything to please Him.

The Novice Mistress took her up the wooden stairs between white walls with texts written on them. Once again her heart beat very fast. She would see her cell at last, or rather 'our cell' as she would have to call it in the Order. None of the Sisters owned anything personally – everything was there to be shared with others. She loved the cell at once. It was the exact opposite of Les Buissonets. Les Buissonets, like the houses of her relatives, was full of heavy mahogany tables and beds and wardrobes. There were enormous chairs with embroidered backs, sofas covered in red plush, golden clocks and candelabra decorated with cherubs and nymphs, embroidered pin cushions preserved under glass cases, glittering chandeliers. Everything was decorated, coloured, stuffed, designed to attract the eye or make the body comfortable.

The cell presented an extraordinary contrast. Both the floor and walls were of bare brown wood, and nothing hung on the walls except a plain cross, a little stoup of holy water, and a portrait of Our Lord. The bed was very narrow with a plain brown cover, and consisted of a straw mattress resting upon boards. Apart from the bed all that the room contained was a stool, a table, a lantern, an hour-glass, and a shelf which held a water jug. Thérèse reflected with pleasure that it was little better than a prisoner's cell – ever since she had prayed for the conversion of the murderer Pranzini[1] she had taken a special interest in prisoners.

The Novice Mistress looked at her few possessions – a pen, a volume of St John of the Cross, a change of dress and of underwear – and said she might keep them for now. She left her for a little while she went to office guessing that Thérèse might want to get used to her new surroundings. At once she went to

the window and found that it looked out on the cloister garth –
she could see the big crucifix in profile, most of the pretty statue
of the Blessed Virgin holding out her arms to welcome her to
Carmel, the flower beds set with rose trees and geraniums, the
grass, the cinder walks. This was her new home. 'I shall be here
for ever and ever' she said to herself. She said it jubilantly,
knowing it was exactly right for her. She gloated once again over
having her very own cell at last – the fact that it was called 'our
cell' made it all the more thrilling, and she quickly knelt to
thank God for his goodness in bringing her here in the face of so
much opposition.

The bell was sounding for the midday meal in refectory. Now
was the time to start being a nun. She went down the stairs,
found the line outside the refectory where the Sisters waited in
twos; she joined the end of it. Inside they sat on one side only of
two long wooden tables so that they faced each other across the
room. There were twenty-five nuns. She was a little surprised to
discover how old most of them were. The only novice was about
eight years older than herself. Then came Pauline and Marie,
both in their thirties, then nuns in their forties and fifties, and
finally several really old nuns. Like the stairs and passages the
refectory had white walls with texts written upon them. 'The
bread of eternal life' was one of them. There was also a skull to
remind you of your mortality. One of the Sisters wore a chipped
cup on a piece of leather round her neck and Thérèse looked at
her with pity knowing that she must be the culprit who broke it.
She wished she could wear it herself.

In front of each Sister was a napkin, a piece of bread, a jug of
water, a bowl and a knife. The Sisters, having folded back their
long sleeves, arranged the napkin in a complicated way between
their plate and their habit to prevent any crumb or drop falling
to the floor. Thérèse tried to copy this until she saw the Novice
Mistress gently shake her head. She bowed to the Sister who
poured her soup, who bowed back. The soup tasted of vegetables, but also as if it had been a little burned. Now she would
eat mostly fruit, vegetables and fish. Meat, eggs, and dairy foods
were forbidden for most of the year except when the Sisters were

sick. When she had finished she cleaned the bowl with her bread as she saw the others do, then wiped it with the napkin.

After the midday meal there was a period of silent prayer. Thérèse prayed joyfully, her heart full of gratitude. Then she was sent out into the garden to do some weeding. She had never cared for weeding at home – Papa or the gardener did that – and enthusiastic as she was, she still found it rather boring, but it gave her a chance to see more of the garden. She worked near the chestnut walk, a pretty avenue between two rows of tall chestnut trees where the Sisters took their recreation on warm summer afternoons.

Later that evening the feelings of homesickness came. About now – on the other side of Lisieux – Papa, Céline and Léonie would be sitting down to supper, doubtless shedding a few tears as they spoke of her. God asked hard things of those who loved Him. But on the other hand she had sat beside Pauline at recreation as the Sisters sat around with their sewing and it had been wonderful to have her so close, to be able to tell her what she was thinking, instead of having to write her a letter or mumble it through the grille. It was lovely too to be back with Marie – her sister/godmother – Marie always gave you a feeling of confidence.

Thérèse could see that her sisters were respected in the convent. She still felt shy of the other twenty-four nuns – she had always been nervous of strangers and known that she seemed quaint and odd to them however hard she tried to be normal – but they had talked so nicely at recreation and everyone had made a point of welcoming her so kindly that she thought that in this holy place maybe her old problems would not recur.

She loved the quietness of the Great Silence, the time when, according to monastic custom, silence was kept from Vespers until after Mass the next morning. Even the name of it had always appealed to her and sometimes she and Céline had practised having a great silence at home just for the pleasure of it, going speechless to bed and not saying a word until Papa returned from Mass next morning. She went to bed in the dusk, lying down at last on a pallet, rustling, narrow and hard. She

liked the smell of the straw. There were no sheets, just woollen
blankets, a woollen pillow, and a heavy blanket of felt. She said
her final prayers, thanking God for bringing her here, and
folded her arms in a cross across her breasts.

She woke once or twice that night, because of the hardness of
the bed and because she was so excited. It was half-light again
when she heard an extraordinary sound – the clatter of castanets
up and down the passages outside. She knew that she was
supposed to get up at once and she did so with only a little
struggle; she would have preferred to stay in bed and think
about the pleasure of being where she was. She washed in the
cold water, dressed herself, and went out into the corridor which
was full of the shuffle of sandals as the nuns made their way
down to choir. She sat in the seat indicated by the Novice
Mistress and tried to wake herself up enough to concentrate on
the office. Again she thought joyfully 'I am here for always,
always' and felt sorry for those in the world outside who could
not know such joy.

After breakfast she was set to do some sweeping. She swept
the passages and the stairs, slowly – she had never done any
sweeping at home and she thought how amused the Martin
maid, Victoire, would be to see her now. In the middle of it
Reverend Mother came along and said 'Hurry up, child. You'll
never get it done at that rate. You look as if you've never swept a
floor before in your life!' With a feeling of excitement that this
was mortification at last Thérèse knelt and kissed the stair.

Reverend Mother sent for Thérèse later in the day. Thérèse
thought she looked unwell.

'You are very young to be here,' she said in her usual sharp
voice, 'but you showed a determination beyond your years.
However, you will find it much harder than you expect. I notice
that your sisters still tend to treat you very much as a child – as
the baby of the family. That is not how I shall treat you. If you
are old enough to test your vocation here, and if we find that you
have a vocation, then you are old enough to be treated like
everyone else.'

The words stung a little. Others had said that she was a

spoiled child, but she had never thought so. All the same, she nodded her head. She did want to be treated like everyone else.

When she saw Pauline and Marie later in the day she noticed that they did tend to fuss. Had she slept well? Was she tired by all the excitement? Did she find the work difficult? Was she hungry? It was irksome to be treated like a piece of porcelain.

Much of her day was spent with the Novice Mistress who was going through the Rule with her, teaching her what a nun was supposed to do with her eyes, feet, hands. She had found out all about the Rule when Pauline had gone to the Carmel, and she and Céline had played at things like 'custody of the eyes' – keeping one's eyes directed to the ground, ignoring interesting sights as a form of detachment – so it was not very new to her. It was hard to remember so many things at once, though, especially as Reverend Mother or the Novice Mistress rebuked you sharply if you got it wrong.

Then there were all the complications of the office book. 'It will take a while to work that out,' the Sister said. Since about four hours a day were spent singing offices, in addition to Mass, she felt bewildered quite a lot of the time.

She suspected that work would turn out to be a bigger problem than the Rule or being in choir, however. Sister Marie of the Angels checked that she really had weeded the flower-bed, and really had swept the stairs. 'Good, but slow' was her verdict. 'You'll have to speed up quite a lot.' Then she took her to the linen room and introduced her to the Sister in charge there.

'Can you sew well, child?' she wanted to know.

'I can hardly sew at all!' Thérèse replied faintly. The Sister was furious.

'Why do they always send me completely useless people?' she wanted to know.

'I am sorry I am useless,' Thérèse said. 'I will try hard,' but this didn't seem to mollify Sister, who had a big pile of torn linen beside her. She made Thérèse do some hemming. She did her very best, but when she had finished Sister said the stitches were far too big and made her unpick it and start again.

'Didn't your mother teach you anything?' she asked unkindly.

Then, it must have occurred to her that Thérèse had no mother, and she looked sorry, but Thérèse felt hurt at the implied criticism of her sisters. Why hadn't they taught her to sew? Probably because she had complained so much that it bored her. The Novice Mistress had also told her that she had not made her bed properly and had made her go back to do it again. At home Céline nearly always made the bed for her. When, on rare occasions, she did it herself, she expected thanks and praise from her sisters for this extraordinary feat. Times had changed!

She found the Novice Mistress Sister Marie of the Angels a bit of a puzzle. Since she had to spend much of her day with her she was the sister she was beginning to know the best, apart from Marie and Pauline, and she noticed that Sister Marie was, there was no other word for it, a bit of a chatterbox. Once she had begun to talk about something she went on and on, slipping in asides and ideas that had just popped into her head. It was as if being silent for most of her waking days gave her an irrepressible need to talk once she had started. Thérèse didn't mind being scolded by her – she just kissed the floor and that was that. What she found much more painful was being expected to be open about her spiritual life. Sister would ask some question about her prayers, what she did in the silence, how she thought about God or Jesus or the Blessed Virgin, and she would listen in a kind of unbelieving astonishment to what Thérèse said in reply. Thérèse knew that Sister probably thought her affected, or that she had made the answers up, and as a result she got more and more shy of talking about her religious feelings and would blush and stammer as soon as the questions began. It was really torture.

Her life was full of consolations, however. Papa wrote every day to his queen, and sometimes Céline and Léonie wrote too. In any case they all came once a week to talk to her through the grille. Papa was always bringing presents and when he did not come himself he sent them – wonderful fish, cherries, apples, plums, pears, vegetables and flowers. The Sister who operated the tourière, the revolving hatch through which objects were passed in and out of the convent, complained jokingly of overwork.

No doubt Papa feared that the convent food would not tempt the fussy palate of his youngest little girl. In truth she was suffering from indigestion and did not feel like eating very much. She wished he wouldn't send the food. It was very loving of him, but it made her feel rather silly.

In May the Jesuit Père Pichon[2] came to the convent for the profession of her sister Marie, Sister Marie of the Sacred Heart, and it turned out to be a very important meeting for Thérèse, as he seemed to be a rare twin soul. They had a long conversation during which he heard her confession. She told him a great deal, though with difficulty since recently she had become so tongue-tied in talking about her inner life. She told of her old problems with scruples (the obsessional worries about her sinfulness), of how she had always felt afraid that she would somehow disgrace her baptism and disappoint her Lord; she explained about her problem with the Novice Mistress.

She found it very consoling that he really listened to her, that he told her that he believed God was doing a remarkable work with her soul – he had watched her praying the previous evening in the choir and had been struck by the simplicity of her childlike fervour. He solemnly assured her that she had never committed a mortal sin, that although she had it in her to be a 'little demon' God's mercy had kept her on the path of love. Finally he reminded her that Novice masters, and mistresses, were fallible creatures but that she had only to remember there was one supreme Novice Master, Jesus, and she needed only to please Him. She went away feeling deeply reassured, as if she had spoken to Jesus himself.

Another reassurance came from one of the old nuns whom she sat beside one day at recreation. 'Dear child, I can't imagine you have a great deal to confide to your superiors,' she said. Knowing how hard she found it to confide in Mother Marie of the Angels, Thérèse was intrigued.

'What makes you say that, Mother?'

'There's such a simplicity about your soul . . . The nearer you approach perfection, the simpler you will become; nearness to God always makes us simple.'[3]

It was comforting to feel herself understood by others, but it did not help her much when once again, having been commanded to talk about her feelings towards God, she was tongue-tied and scarlet with embarrassment.

Sometimes she went to Reverend Mother for spiritual direction. Not very often, because Mother was often ill. Thérèse was puzzled by Reverend Mother's attitude to her. She would hear her being kindness itself to other sisters, and if, say, a priest visited the community she would always say nice things about their little postulant in Thérèse's hearing. Yet whenever they met she would find fault and speak sharply to her, though she tried very hard to please her. She could not understand it.

She mentioned it to Pauline, whose wary, concerned expression did not help her much. She could talk to Pauline, however, as she had always talked since a tiny child, about her religious feelings. Pauline always understood what she meant – she was someone who knew about deep mysteries, in particular the mystery of the Holy Face of Jesus.

She encouraged Thérèse, in some of her free moments, to stand in front of the great crucifix in the cloister garth and look up into the face of the Lord, clouded with suffering, yet so deeply compassionate. Another of Thérèse's devotions was to the little statue of the Child Jesus in the cloister. She felt an immediate attachment to it. With permission she picked flowers, the sort of flowers a child would like – daisies, buttercups and roses – and arranged them in front of the statue. Once she made a daisy chain, just as she and Céline used to do.

She was exploring the nooks and crannies of her new home. There was not very much of it, but then she was allowed very little time to herself. She enjoyed the white candles of the chestnut trees, the red and white tiles of the cloister floor, the long grass of the orchard with its wild flowers and blossoming trees. She was in a beautiful place, so full of peace and quietness. Sometimes all she could hear was a bee buzzing in a flower. But even if it had been noisy and ugly she knew that it was the place where she wanted to be. Uncle Isidore had said that she had a dream of what being a nun would be like and that the reality would be very different. The odd thing was that it was exactly what she expected.

Chapter Two

THE LITTLE QUEEN

Thérèse's mother, Zélie (Azélie-Marie) Guérin had had a wretched childhood. The daughter of a cavalry soldier, she was the second of three children. Neither of her parents showed her any affection – this was reserved entirely for the boy and baby of the family, Isidore – and she became a sort of scapegoat for her mother, in whose eyes she could never do right. Not particularly given to self-pity she complained that her childhood had been 'as sad as a shroud'. She was frequently ill and continually suffered from migraine.

At nineteen she tried to enter the convent of the Sisters of St Vincent de Paul at Alençon. Possibly because of her mother's secret intervention, they refused her.

Frustrated in this first ambition she decided to learn lacemaking, a craft which she had enjoyed at school, in the famous lace-making school of Alençon. *Point d'Alençon* was manufactured by embroidering over a netted base, an elaborate process that made the lace beautiful but costly. After two years' training Zélie set herself up as a professional lacemaker.

Her sister Élise had joined the Poor Clares but became so ill from recurrent pneumonia that she was obliged to leave. Eventually she joined the less rigorous convent of the Visitation nuns at Le Mans. Dosithée, as she was known at Le Mans, would play a very important part in the life of Zélie's family, advising and admonishing her sister about the upbringing of her children, instructing and disciplining the children themselves.

When Zélie was refused by the order of St Vincent de Paul she had at once begun to dream of a different sort of life – of having a big family of children, all so carefully brought up that many of them would choose to be priests, nuns, monks or missionaries.

Her husband-to-be, Louis Martin, was also the child of a soldier, an army captain who had fought in the Russian campaign. Bullied by his father, spoiled by his mother, Louis grew up as a melancholy dreamer, timid and indecisive. Without any inclination to be a soldier, and lacking the brains to be a scholar, he found it hard to find a niche in the world. He was pious, and at twenty he had made the long journey to the Swiss border in the hope of being accepted by the monks of the Great St Bernard. They had gently turned him away for lack of educational accomplishments. Suffering from the set-back he had gone to Strasbourg and studied for two years as a clockmaker, a slow, silent trade that suited his temperament rather well. Back in Alençon again he continued to dream of monastic life, and began studying in an attempt to improve his education but the result of his studies was a nervous breakdown. He went to Paris where, living with his grandmother, he continued his clock-making studies. Years later he was to speak of the 'terrible temptations' of Paris, temptation from which he felt he had been saved by his piety. Perhaps too by his timidity. Returning from Paris he opened a clockmaking and jewellery shop in Alençon.

One day Zélie saw Louis crossing the Pont St Leonard over the Sarthe in Alençon and the Lord put it into her mind that this was the man she would marry. Louis's mother was learning lacemaking, and was able to effect an introduction. She approved of Zélie and she thought it time that her thirty-five-year-old son was married. So, without so far as we know, any strong wish for marriage, Louis was promised to Zélie. Marriage was expected of those not sworn to the religious life, and this unlikely couple, both of whom had had other plans for themselves, got married in July, 1858 in Notre Dame d'Alençon. Zélie was twenty-six.

Zélie's dreams of children had become very real to her, so it must have been a shock to her when, so legend has it, Louis informed her on their wedding night (driven by what state of panic we can only guess) that he proposed they should live together as brother and sister. A 'Josephite marriage' was the term for it in those days, a reference to the tradition that Joseph and Mary never had sexual intercourse.

It was not a marriage entered into with very high expectations of personal happiness on either side yet despite Zélie's initial disappointment the couple continued together in apparent harmony. They were seen daily at Mass in the very early dawn before their respective businesses demanded their attention, they read pious books together and observed the feasts and fasts of the Church's year. The next year, 1859, Josephite marriage or not, Zélie was pregnant with the first of her children, Marie (Marie-Louise) and after this eight children came quickly one after another. Marie was followed by Marie-Pauline (Pauline), Pauline by Marie-Léonie (Léonie), and Léonie by Marie-Hélène, who was to die of consumption at the age of five. Special prayers to St Joseph produced two boys in succession, Marie-Joseph-Louis and Marie-Joseph-Jean Baptiste. Both died before their first birthdays. Then came Marie-Céline, who survived, and Marie-Melanie-Thérèse who died before she was a year old. Infant deaths were common enough at the time. All the same, Zélie felt the pain of her children's deaths bitterly but took comfort in the thought that she would see them again in heaven.

All Zélie's children, even the survivors, suffered acutely in their early years, in particular from enteritis. How far her own state of health contributed to the children's sickliness it is hard to say. For some years Zélie had had a secret, a cancer in her breast, which, though it seemed to grow slowly, was gradually undermining her health.

In 1871, whether because of prosperity or because he always found the world a strain, Louis Martin gave up his clockmaking business and the family went to live at a pretty little house with a small garden in the rue Saint-Blaise which Zélie had inherited from her father. Zélie ran her business from there – preparing designs for outworkers who then brought the work back to her for her to approve – and supervised the household. She was chronically overworked. Louis, though still in middle age, entered into a kind of retirement which would last for the rest of his life. The sale of his business, Zélie's thriving trade, and some inherited money meant that they were fairly well-to-do.

In 1872, forty-one by now, and once again pregnant, Zélie wrote to tell her brother that she was expecting another baby – a boy she felt sure – and that she thought it might come at the end of the year. She was anxious about the delivery, dreading another difficult confinement. Marie-Françoise-Thérèse was born at 11.30 at night on Thursday 2 January. She was a fine child, weighing around eight pounds, whom her mother described as 'gentille'. The birth had been easy and quick. The baby would be baptised the next day, Saturday, and the oldest Martin child Marie, would be her godmother.[4]

It was a happy and hopeful beginning – the birth of a last, cherished, child – but within a month Thérèse was showing signs of gastric illness and was soon near to death. 'The little one is suffering horribly' her distraught mother wrote, agonised that yet another child seemed to be going from her. The sick mother's milk, the doctor thought, was poisoning the baby.

In March, when the baby was around eight weeks old, Zélie sought a wet-nurse, Rose Taillé, who had nursed one of their other sick children. Rose lived at Semallé, a village within easy travelling distance of Alençon. Since she had her own family to care for and the farm to run, she could not go to live with the Martins as Zélie had hoped at first, but offered to take Thérèse under her own roof. For most of the first year of her life, therefore, the baby lived at a farm on the Bocage with her surrogate-mother, seeing her mother and sisters only on Thursdays when Rose came into Alençon to go to market. Thérèse's biographers tend to find this a charming note, imagining the baby girl surrounded by chickens and flowers. The damage to the bonding of mother and baby, now thought to be so important, the trauma of separation to be succeeded by yet another separation when the baby was returned, the intensity of inexpressible feeling, all suggest to a modern reader that this was the first of a series of tragedies that beset Thérèse's childhood, one certainly relevant to some of the psychological pain she suffered later. Thérèse returned home to Alençon in April 1874. She was fifteen months old.

Soon after Thérèse had returned, Zélie painted a poignant picture of 'Baby' in a letter written to Pauline, who was away at school.

Here's Baby coming to stroke my face with her tiny hand and give me a hug. The poor little thing stays with me all the time, and hates being parted from me. She's very fond of going into the garden, but if I'm not there she won't stay in it; she cries till she's brought back to me.[5]

Thérèse could not bear her mother to leave her sight.

Yet the baby Thérèse already showed signs both of deter-mined character and of a lack of physical fear. 'Your father has just put up a swing, and Céline couldn't be happier. But you ought to see Baby swinging: it's so amusing, the grown-up way she sits there, and you can be quite sure that she will hang on to the rope. But soon she starts yelling because it isn't going fast enough, and then she has to be strapped down with another rope in front – even so, it makes me nervous to see her perched up there.'[5]

It was a loving family in which to live. Zélie, although weak-ened by her illness, and spending more time on the couch or in her chair working on lace designs, was still well enough to enjoy her life and her children. Céline, three and a half years older than Thérèse, and a source of boundless admiration for her, was a useful companion. Marie and Pauline, aged thirteen and twelve, played a very active part in looking after the younger children in their holidays from school. The odd one out, then as later, was Léonie. Not as pretty as her sisters, physically awk-ward and slow at lessons, she had a kind of obstinacy which Zélie felt to be a challenge to her authority. Léonie, although a religious child who loved Bible stories and had a real faith of her own, would not spend the time in private prayer that her mother prescribed, nor follow little disciplines designed to make her a 'good child'. Overreacting, Zélie seemed to fear that Léonie might be damned, and openly wondered once whether it would have been better if she had died during one of her childhood illnesses. Taking their note from her, the rest of the family, so emotionally involved with one another, seemed always to leave Léonie out, or to ridicule her clumsy comments, or to speak of her only in tones of exasperation as 'poor Léonie' without even noticing they did it. Her loneliness must have been intense, and the more intense because of the patent 'goodness' of everyone connected with her. If they were good then she must be bad.

Thérèse clung to Zélie, but her special passion was for Papa. Louis, who was given to extravagant names for his daughters – Marie was his diamond, Pauline his pearl – gave the most extravagant of all to his youngest. Thérèse was 'the little queen', or 'the queen of France and Navarre' (to which she riposted by always calling him 'the king' or 'the king of France and Navarre'). Perhaps because she was the last child, or maybe for quite other reasons, Thérèse seemed to open wells of tenderness and love in Louis's rather repressed nature that none of his other children had discovered. When Zélie protested, with truth, that he was spoiling the child outrageously, he replied simply 'But she is the queen!' as if he half believed his own fantasy.[6] Neither Zélie nor the other children doubted that he loved Thérèse before them all, but, as sometimes happens in families, they transmuted their jealousy by themselves heaping love upon the favoured one.

Thus Thérèse was always the centre of attention, her charming babyish sayings and doings a matter of continual delight within the family, written down so that the girls away at school should know all about it. Her mother's letters tell us that Thérèse is clever and original ('perhaps the cleverest of all of you'), that she is good and sweet as an angel. 'She has a blonde head and a golden heart, and is very tender and candid.'[7] 'The dear little one is our sunshine. She is going to be wonderfully good; the germ of goodness can already be seen.'[8]

The fondest hope of Zélie and Louis was that their daughter would turn out to be a 'little saint'. 'I ask the Holy Virgin', Zélie wrote to her sister-in-law in words that seemed to acknowledge her approaching death, 'that all the little girls she has given me may become saints, and that I may be permitted to follow their destinies from close by.'[9]

So, the education of Thérèse and her sisters, though loving and tender, with many hugs and kisses, was concentrated on making them good. Good children, they soon learned, went to heaven, which was a place much better than this earth. Bad children went to hell. The first words that Thérèse was taught to recite were pious verses depicting the place above the bright blue sky. At the appropriate words Baby had learned to turn her eyes heavenwards, a trick that delighted servants and relatives. 'We never tire of having her repeat this, it's so charming! There is something so heavenly in her look that it quite carries us away.'[10]

Thérèse was a very precocious child, bright, lively, funny and touching. She is described alternately as an imp, an urchin, and a monkey. She was bravely obstinate, particularly perhaps in the face of the insensitive punishments visited upon children of the period. 'When she says "no" nothing can make her change, and she can be terribly obstinate. You could keep her down in the cellar all day without getting a "yes" out of her; she would rather sleep there.'[11] This suggests a considerable conflict between Thérèse and her mother, one which Thérèse was winning.

The child was truthful, almost excessively so. Picking up the family's enthusiasm for penitence and for asking for forgiveness, she managed almost to caricature it, pushing and smacking Céline and then insisting on instant confession, tearing the wallpaper and making sure her father was informed the minute he got home.

Quite soon, however, there was fear beneath all this struggle for goodness, fear of losing Zélie's love, and fear of having committed a mortal sin. Thérèse, acutely observant, noticed how sharp and unkind Zélie could be with Léonie who had difficulty in joining the family's taste for penitence. Zélie gave Léonie a number of cork pieces, one of which she was supposed to put in a drawer every time she did something wrong; Léonie refused to play this game and Zélie was distraught at her refusal, imagining that it revealed sinful pride or worse. Zélie also worried whether her dead daughter Marie-Hélène, who had told some little fib before she died at the age of five, would be damned for it. Thérèse was so awed by all of this that, according to her mother, she would not tell a fib to save her life.

Thérèse had other faults, though, which her family treated half seriously, half with amusement. They noted that she was quite vain about her appearance and loved to admire herself in the glass in a pretty dress as little girls do. After this they took care never to tell her she was pretty, but on the contrary said she was ugly, presumably regarding this as a lie in a good cause.

She was given to tantrums and tears of rage and sometimes she 'back-answered' her father whom her sisters thought was far too lenient in letting his little queen order him about. She had a strong sense of her own dignity. Once Zélie said she would give her a sou if she would kiss the floor the way nuns did when they committed a fault in the convent. (This, like so much else in Zélie's way of managing her family, reveals her ambition to make life in the home as much like life in a convent as possible. Not surprisingly, it was around this age that Thérèse first declared that she would be a nun when she grew up.) A sou was a small fortune to the little girl, but Thérèse refused indignantly. It would be good to think that Zélie felt rebuked by the child's integrity, but there is no evidence that she did. She tells the story with some amusement in one of her letters.

Thérèse and Céline had become inseparable friends. Rose Taillé had presented the children with a couple of white bantams – a cock and a hen – and Thérèse remarked that she and Céline could no more bear to be parted than could the cock and the hen. The children would bring the chickens indoors and sit cuddling them before the fire for hours.

When Céline was six she had a string of movable beads that Marie had brought home from her convent school – a special sort of rosary – on which she was taught to move a bead every time she made a 'sacrifice'. 'Sacrifices' meant letting others win games, or doing small jobs around the house when you would rather be playing. Thérèse, then three, had to have one too. She kept it in the pocket of her apron and Zélie delighted to see her little hand go into the pocket to move a bead when she thought she was being unselfish.

At three years old, a time of chaotic emotion in most children, the practice seems forced and unnatural. Thérèse's priest biographers were full of enthusiasm. 'From the beginning there was a happy tendency towards restraint, reticence, renunciation, recollection in all senses.'[12] Thérèse herself believed that her iron self-control came naturally to her. Yet her mother's letters paint quite a different picture, a much more normal one.

Baby, when things aren't going well for her, gets pitiably worked up, so that I have to talk her round; she seems to think that all is lost, and sometimes the feeling is too much for her, and she chokes with indignation. She's such a very excitable child . . .[13]

The weapon used against her natural wishes – that God would be displeased with her – was an overwhelmingly powerful one in a household in which God was the only thing that mattered. 'When she was still very small', her sister Marie remembered, 'it was necessary only to say to her . . . "That offends God." '[14] 'Since the age of three,' said Thérèse of herself, 'I have refused God nothing.'

Soon she developed a rather pitiable habit of asking, whenever she did anything at all, whether it would please Jesus or displease him, the thought of displeasing him being a source of boundless anxiety to her. At five she had a habit of asking when Pauline put her to bed whether she had been good that day, and whether God was pleased with her. 'I always got the answer "Yes". I would have cried all night otherwise.'[15] Sleep was impossible if she had neglected to say her prayers.

If a childhood lived so remorselessly in the atmosphere of 'sin', and 'being good' imposed heavy anxieties, it also provided its own poetry. Louise and Zélie went out at 5.30 every morning to Mass and the children longed to be old enough to share the privilege too. The family dressed itself for the pleasure of Sunday and of going to Mass, and, unusually among the townspeople, Zélie and Louis both refused to do business on Sundays, so that the day could be entirely devoted to God and to the family. They walked together, sang, visited relatives. The seasons of the Church's year brought their own especial joys, with flowers and processions and special prayers and hymns.

In May, the month of Mary, she for whom all of the children were named, they built an altar in the home right up to the ceiling with fruit blossoms and greenery. Zélie was very particular about how this was done, as she was about all else. 'Mama is very hard to satisfy', Thérèse significantly sighed once. 'Much harder than God's Mother!' On Sundays, when Thérèse was still tiny, she was left at home with Louise the maid while the others went to church. They would return with some 'pain bénit' (consecrated bread) for the stay-at-homes, which was received by Thérèse with rapturous excitement. Once when Céline left it behind at church, the two children consecrated a bit of home-made bread themselves and found, mysteriously, that it tasted just the same.

In Thérèse's earliest years Marie and Pauline were away at school – at the Convent of the Visitation at Le Mans. Once Thérèse and Zélie travelled there by train, just the two of them, partly to visit the girls, partly to visit Aunt Dosithée. Aunt had prepared a white sugar mouse as a treat, and a little basket of sweets which included two rings made of sugar, one, Thérèse decided, for herself, and one for Céline. To her distress the sweets, including one of the rings, dropped out of the basket on the way home, an accident that caused her a lot of distress.

The highlights of the younger children's lives were when the big girls returned for the holidays. Pauline, Thérèse's favourite, always brought a stick of chocolate for her, sweeping the little girl up in her arms for hugs. Thérèse loved to play with Pauline's long plaits.

Marie, the oldest of the sisters, suffered terribly from scruples, partly from her mother's continually questioning her as to whether she had committed any 'fault' and thus driven God from her heart. At eight, when she went as a boarder to the Visitation convent, Aunt Dosithée noted that she was 'melancholy'. She cannot have been made any more cheerful by Aunt Dosithée's methods. Seeing that the little girl wept a lot from homesickness, she refused to cuddle or kiss her until she stopped crying. Marie loved her aunt and was devastated by this punishment. Soon after Thérèse was born Marie fell into a severe, mysterious fever, probably hysterical in origin. A mixture of envy of the baby coupled with despair at her own tormented existence may have been responsible.

Pauline, the second of the Martin daughters, was Zélie's favourite, and the one who most closely resembled her. Pauline was a strong, practical, assertive person, whom her sisters often called 'Paulin', as if she was the boy of the family. More extravert than Marie her youthful problems had more to do with social adjustment than with self-doubt. It troubled Pauline that, unlike most of her schoolmates at the Visitation, she was not nobly born, that the Martins did not live as luxuriously as others, and that she was rather small for her age.

Léonie, uncooperative and given to fits of rage, was Zélie's despair. The maid Louise was taken on with the express purpose of controlling the rebellious and unhappy little girl, and succeeded at the cost of terrorising poor Léonie. Aunt Dosithée had two attempts at taking over the care of Léonie, perhaps as much to give Zélie a rest as anything. Desperately sick in infancy, given to accidents in which she hurt herself badly, painfully slow at learning anything, driven to fury by all attempts at discipline, Léonie was a continual source of worry and grievance to Zélie.

Céline, by contrast, was a sunny, physically active, perhaps rather unimaginative child, seemingly without problems, the most stable of the Martin children.

From when Thérèse was about three her mother's long illness began to take a turn for the worse. Perhaps because of this Marie stayed home from school and began to take over some of the duties of the household, including teaching Céline. Thérèse, who hated to be parted from Céline, sat in on these lessons, often bored, sleepy and tearful but determined not to miss anything. Perhaps because she was brighter than Céline she quite quickly began to learn herself.

Léonie decided one day that she was too old to play with dolls any longer and she produced a basket of dolls' clothes with stuff for making other little dresses and told the two little girls that they might choose whatever they liked. Céline, like a well brought up child, chose some pretty braid, but Thérèse, whole-heartedly, said 'I choose the whole lot!', a story which would often be retold in the Martin family. Writing about this rather charming act of greed nearly twenty years later Thérèse saw it as the key to her whole life. She was one who wanted everything, and because she wanted everything she wanted God, and the total surrender of self which she saw as the road to God.

Even at three or four she thought and talked of God continually, picking up the habit of the Martin household. When Céline asked how God could fit into something as tiny as the Host Thérèse was heard to explain that since He was Almighty he could do anything. With the sort of precocity that Zélie and the big girls fostered in them the two children worked out a 'Rule of Life' for themselves (a plan about prayer, mortification and attendance at the Mass) to the amazement of a local shop-keeper who overheard them talking about it in the grocer's.

'What *are* they talking about?' she exclaimed in astonishment.

They were also encouraged to give money to beggars they met on the road – Thérèse was dismayed one day when a man on crutches she thought she was being kind to refused her offer with some indignation. She realised that she had hurt his feelings.

There was something more than a little precious about all this self-conscious practice of religion. Thérèse, recalling her three-to four-year-old self, says that 'I always made a point of not complaining when things were taken away from me and when I was blamed for something I hadn't done, I held my tongue instead of making excuses.'[16] Already at three she is living in the atmosphere of the convent.

Not surprisingly she was finding it hard to mix with children outside the family. Sometimes she and Céline played with the *préfet's* daughter, a wealthy child with lovely toys and a big garden. But Thérèse preferred it when she and Céline stayed at home and played with each other, scraping bits of shiny stone off the garden walls, pretending they were valuable, and selling them to Papa.

Her life was an odd mixture of security in a home in which everyone was devoted to her (it obviously rankled a bit, though, that the maid, Louise, frankly preferred Céline) and deeper feelings of the utmost terror. These centred upon hell, and she suffered at least one bad dream in which she saw demons dancing in the garden.

Some of Thérèse's distress came from her child's perception that her mother was desperately ill. With iron self-control Zélie carried on with life as usual for as long as she could, but during the last eighteen months of her life she was in too much pain to run her business or her family. Marie and Pauline took over the reins of the household, teaching and caring for the little ones.

A comment of Thérèse to her mother when aged about three and a half, 'I wish you would die so that you could go to heaven', has been hailed as a sign of the future saint's otherworldly vision. It is possible to think of much more mundane explanations – that the child was, rather archly, parroting back the underlying statement of her family's way of life, or, more tragically, that she was, tentatively, asking whether her mother was going to live, in the oblique, frightened way that children do sometimes ask such important questions. Or it might be that the sight of her mother's long-drawn out suffering, even when partly concealed from the child, was a potent source of distress and what she meant was 'If you are going to die, die, because I cannot bear seeing you suffer, nor the suspense of wondering whether I am going to lose you.'

Certainly for two years before she died of cancer Zélie Martin was seriously ill. She had discussed her symptoms with her brother, the chemist, Isidore Guérin, as long before her death as 1864. With enormous determination she had carried on life as usual for as long as she possibly could, but eventually she moved to a room away from the rest of the family – where any cries could not be heard. She continued to go regularly to early Mass and Sunday Mass, though often she needed to be physically supported. In June 1877 she made a pilgrimage to Lourdes with the three older girls hoping for a miracle but came home to begin the final stage of her illness. Even then she did not expect to die soon, maybe feeling that her iron will would keep her alive. It took Isidore to inform her rather bravely one night at dinner that she would be dead within the month and that she needed to prepare herself. Towards the end she became acutely, agonisingly, sensitive to sound, movement and loud voices, probably because she was in terrible pain, pain too great to allow her to lie in bed. She continually dragged herself up to walk about the room.

Little children are not usually as ignorant of painful facts as grown-ups choose to believe, though they may pretend to know less than they do, but a child of Thérèse's intelligence must have observed much and feared acutely what was coming. She was kept away from her mother in a way that she was not used to, and when she was with her she could perceive all too clearly how changed she was, how she could no longer take her in her arms, or even smile, except with difficulty.

Thérèse, who had suffered two dislocations in her young life – one from her mother soon after birth, the other from her surrogate-mother of a year – was broken by the shock of her mother's death when it came.

Days before the death, the two youngest children were kept away from Zélie, sent off to stay with neighbours and play with their children while knowing about the crisis that waited at home. Once Céline took home an apricot that a neighbour had given her having kept it as a present for her mother, but Zélie was too ill to eat it. All five of the daughters knelt in Zélie's bedroom when she received Extreme Unction, Louis weeping as loudly as any of them. On 28 August 1877, Zélie Martin died.

When she was dead Louis picked up Thérèse in his arms so that she could kiss the cold forehead. A great loneliness came upon the child. She crept away to crouch in a lonely corridor and found herself overshadowed by a gigantic piece of wood – the lid of the coffin, as she gradually realised. 'I hated the size of it,' she says. A kind of hopelessness about life seized her. She consoled her four-year-old self by thinking of a heaven 'so joyful, with all my trials over, the winter of my soul for ever past.' In the spring of that year Zélie had written to Pauline of Thérèse, 'Her disposition is so good. She is a chosen spirit.'[17]

Chapter Three

BORN FOR GREATNESS

Thérèse was deeply affected by Zélie's death. The child who had shown a merry, outgoing disposition, changed overnight.

I, who had been so lively, so communicative, was now a shy and quiet little girl, and over-sensitive. Merely to be looked at made me burst into tears; I was only happy when nobody paid any attention to me; I hated having strange people about, and could only recover my good spirits when I was alone with the family.[18]

A very moving scene followed Zélie's funeral. Upon Louise making some sentimental remark that the poor little mites no longer had a mother, Céline threw herself into the arms of Marie saying 'Then you've got to be Mamma.' Thérèse immediately followed suit with the sister she loved most dearly – 'My Mamma's going to be Pauline.' Léonie, caught between the older and younger children, as usual stood alone.

Zélie's death brought about another marked change in the life of the children. Uncle Isidore and Aunt Céline lived at Lisieux, and feeling that his children would need the guiding hand of a woman, Louis moved to Lisieux, to a house called Les Buissonets. It was a delightful house for a growing family, bigger than the one in Alençon and surrounded by a pleasant garden with many trees (the name of the house means 'little shrubbery'). In spite of their grief the children were excited by the change. The whole family set off for Lisieux arriving at the Guérin household at nightfall where their cousins Jeanne and Marie were standing at the door looking out for them. The Martins' brief stay with the Guérins while their own house was got ready made Thérèse very fond of her cousins and enchanted by their prettiness, though a little frightened of Uncle Isidore.

At Les Buissonets a whole new life began for the stricken family, as they drew together to comfort themselves for the loss of Zélie. Léonie, as usual, was cut out of the charmed circle going off as a boarder to the Benedictine school which later Céline and Thérèse would attend as day-girls. Doubtless grieving herself for the loss of her mother she had to do her grieving among strangers while her sisters drew ever closer together without her.

Pauline really did take over the role of Thérèse's mother, inheriting some of the formidable strength of character that Zélie had shown. She dressed Thérèse in the morning, helping her say her prayers. Then Marie and Pauline alternately taught the two little girls – reading, catechism, bible history. Thérèse was a good reader, but tended to grow tearful over the mechanics of grammar. Pauline often showed her pictures, usually of a pious kind, and one of these, significantly, was called 'A little flower at the door of the Tabernacle.' Somehow she identified with this flower, so patiently offering itself to Jesus.

She loved romantic tales, particularly if they had a religious tinge. She was particularly fired by the story of Joan of Arc. She was very excited at the idea of glory – 'gloire'. 'I felt that I was born for greatness.' She decided that the only way she was likely to achieve this was by becoming 'a great saint'.

In this she and Pauline were in accord. Moulding a saint was very much to the taste of Zélie's daughter. Surrogate-motherhood was, in many ways, an onerous job for a seventeen-year-old, one which Pauline's natural capability and undoubted gift for teaching made light of. Although a good teacher she does seem to have been rather doctrinaire, more so than Zélie would have been, maybe from a wish not to betray Zélie's dying trust in her.

It also seems likely that, alongside her warm love for her little sister, Pauline found it fascinating to try out her theories on religion and upbringing on a real child. Thérèse, so bright, so obliging, was treated as a mixture of pet and doll. When she came to write her autobiography she seemed so excessively grateful to Pauline, so lavish in her praise, so incapable of entertaining even a breath of criticism, that after a while the reader begins to wonder whether Thérèse is suppressing doubts that she might, in part, have been a victim. But when a sister has sacrificed precious years of her youth to standing in for a lost mother, and when love is, in a sense, the only permitted attitude, it is difficult to admit resentment, in this case resentment at an education that made Thérèse quaint, unchildlike, and painfully anxious about her sins.

Pauline worked out an educational system in which she gave Thérèse 'marks' – wooden tokens – for each piece of work properly done. Sometimes she gave 'special marks' for outstanding work and enough of these entitled Thérèse to a whole holiday. On an ordinary day she went off to show Papa her five marks in his room at the top of the house and that meant that the two of them were free to go for an outing in the afternoon. If she didn't get the five marks then Pauline would not let her go.

Papa's idea of a walk was not to visit swings or other places of childish delight but to go and pray quietly in one of the town's churches. That way Thérèse got to know most of the local churches. But he remembered to buy a tiny present for the 'little queen' on the way home, a cake or some sweets.

After the walk she played in the garden, mixing 'tisanes' of her own invention from seeds and bits of bark which she then made Papa drink from a doll's cup. Gardening, of the busy kind which makes it hard for anything to grow, was another of her pleasures. She also liked arranging flowers on tiny altars she had built around the garden. Dolls did not figure much in her playing. Ida Görres, one of Thérèse's more perceptive biographers, makes the interesting suggestion that maybe mothering was too painful now that Thérèse lacked her own mother. She did not wish to be reminded.

Occasionally she and her father went fishing together, carrying jam sandwiches cut by Pauline. Thérèse didn't much enjoy the actual fishing, but preferred sinking into a sort of meditative trance, among the flowers and birds. 'Earth', she says, in a most unchildlike way, 'seemed a place of exile, and I could dream of heaven.' Maybe it was a plan to rejoin Zélie.

Pauline worked hard at being a substitute-mother. She not only looked like Zélie but she had her firmness of character, and her steadfastness. Thérèse knew exactly where she stood with her; if she forbad something it remained forbidden. Thérèse had become frightened of the dark, but Pauline devised a sort of aversion therapy getting the little girl by degrees to go and fetch things from dark rooms until her fear gradually evaporated.

Once Thérèse was very rude to the servant Victoire and hurt her feelings by calling her 'une petite mioche' (a little brat) which was what Victoire was fond of calling her. Under pressure Thérèse apologised but twenty years later she remembered that she had not really been sorry because she felt Victoire had deserved it.

At six Thérèse made her first confession to a curate called M. Ducellier. Pauline had prepared her very carefully for it, making sure she understood that it was God to whom she was confessing her sins. Well-primed, Thérèse went into the confessional only to discover that she was so small that the priest did not notice she was there. At his suggestion she made her confession standing up and he then gave her a little talk about devotion to the Blessed Virgin, to which she listened with great care.

Once M. Ducellier came on a visit when only Thérèse and Victoire were at home, so he came into the kitchen and had a chat with Thérèse and a look at her school-books, which made her feel very pleased with herself.

Pauline was good at explaining the Christian mysteries as the various feasts came round. Thérèse's favourite was Corpus Christi when she could throw rose petals at the altar. The best day of all was Sunday, however. It began with Pauline bringing her her chocolate in bed as a treat, and then she was beautifully dressed up and her hair was curled with the curling tongs. 'It was a very happy little girl who went downstairs to put her hand in Papa's and be greeted with a specially loving kiss in honour of the day; and then we all went off to High Mass.'[19]

The king and queen of France and Navarre held hands all the

way to the cathedral and then insisted on sitting together once they had got there. Maybe Thérèse, who had quite a lot of the actress in her, found something sentimentally romantic in the occasion. 'People seemed so impressed by the sight of this fine old man and his tiny daughter . . .'[20]

Thérèse tried hard to understand the sermons. If ever her namesake, Teresa of Avila, was mentioned, Papa used to admonish 'Listen carefully, little queen; this is about your patron saint.'[21] Thérèse did listen carefully.

Except when he was playing with Thérèse Louis seemed very melancholy these days. She noticed that his eyes were quite often filled with tears.

Sundays were such a delight that she began to feel sad towards the end of the afternoon walks, reflecting that the day would soon be over and tomorrow it would be back to boring lessons again. Marie or Pauline often spent Sunday evenings at the Guérins. Occasionally Thérèse did too, but she was still quite scared of Uncle Isidore, of his habit of asking her a lot of questions, or of sitting her on his knee while he sang a song about Bluebeard.

Going home in the starry night she found a constellation that looked like a T, and rather coyly insisted to Louis that her name was written in heaven. Even more tiresomely she resolved that she 'wasn't going to waste any more time looking at an ugly thing like the earth'.

The winter evenings were great fun – there were games of draughts, and Papa singing to the little ones in a fine voice, or reciting poetry to them. Thérèse was impressed at Louis's appearance at family prayers – 'you had only to watch him to see what Saints are like when they pray.' The sisters kissed him goodnight formally, starting with the oldest and working down to the youngest. In order for Thérèse to be kissed he had to lift her up by the elbows and she would be so excited that she would shout goodnight at him.

In bed on winter nights she often felt afraid of the dark, but thanks to Pauline's cure she gradually got over this and the dark never frightened her again. During winter colds and summer fevers Pauline nursed her very devotedly. Once when Thérèse was in bed and feeling ill Pauline gave her her own prized mother-of-pearl pocket-knife to cheer her up. 'If I was dying,' Thérèse once asked Pauline dramatically, 'would you give me your watch to save me?' 'Save your life? I'd give it to you at once if it just made you feel better!' Such remarks gave Thérèse deep reassurance.

Pauline received her confidences and her doubts and resolved the most complicated theological questions that Thérèse could think up. Thérèse, rather revealingly, wondered why God did not give the same amount of glory to all the elect when they got to heaven. Didn't it make some of them unhappy to be less glorious than others? (Shades of childhood envy.) Pauline filled a drinking-mug and Thérèse's little thimble with water and asked which was the fuller? Thérèse had to admit that they were both full, and Pauline explained that each soul was given as much of God's glory as it could contain.

Not all Pauline's teaching methods were quite so straightforward. Ida Görres quotes a hot and tired little Thérèse begging Pauline for a drink.

And Pauline would reply: 'How would you like to save a poor sinner by giving up your drink?' With a heavy sigh the child nods. The big sister is so touched by this willingness that after a while she comes to Thérèse with a glass full of water. Puzzled, Thérèse asks whether she will not harm the sinner if she drinks after all. No, Pauline suggests; first you gave him the merit of your sacrifice; now you can help him by your obedience.[22]

On the surface the child has been taught a lesson in self-control. Behind that, however, is a whole doctrine of substitutive suffering, one that it is impossible for Thérèse to check in any way. If she suffers, so the admired Pauline claims, then some one else will be saved. How can she be such a monster as to choose *not* to suffer? The blow to her self-esteem would be too great. It is only a short step from this to choosing to suffer in *every* situation with a vague feeling that this is what love demands. Zélie and Pauline might have felt that this was the end-result they sought to produce; in a child as willing and sensitive as Thérèse, who had seen the way Léonie was punished for *not* accepting this harsh regime, it was not very difficult to train her in this way. But it produced bewilderment in Thérèse. Since she must drink and eat and have her own way sometimes, how could she know when those times were? And since it was painful to have needs which were not met, it was easier to learn to repress the needs themselves. From there it was but a short step to losing touch with the needs altogether, simply not knowing any more whether one was thirsty or hungry or tired. Simultaneously this brought a loss of contact with the inner self and its requirements. Thus, the 'higher self', as Pauline might have thought of it, the self that insists on rigid self-control, becomes the enemy of the 'lower self' with its insistence on survival. The higher self begins to see the body, with its natural appetites, as 'the enemy', to which the body responds with mute rage and, sooner or later, with symptoms. Pauline, however innocently, was, we may think, embarking on a dangerous game.

'I cannot remember,' says Pauline (Mère Agnes) in her deposition at Thérèse's canonisation, 'that she was disobedient to me a single time. In all things she asked for permission, and when I refused she sometimes cried, but she obeyed without ever insisting on having her way.' The obedient nun was well on her way to being formed.

Fortunately there were more childlike episodes. When Thérèse was seven or eight her father took the family to the seaside, to Trouville. Thérèse had never seen the sea before and was immensely excited by it. She was running about on the sand when a couple asked M. Martin if that pretty little girl was his daughter. Thérèse, always self-conscious, and more than a little fascinated by the picture she made, was secretly delighted, though Louis frowned and made it clear that he did not want them showering compliments upon her. For Thérèse it was confirmation of a secret belief she already held about herself, that she was pretty, if not actually beautiful. Having carefully regaled the incident in *The Story of a Soul* she goes on to say that she wasn't really interested in the admiring looks the lady gave her, because she 'never took any notice of what other people said, except you (Pauline) and Papa'. It is a piece of disingenuousness. What the grown-up Thérèse thought she ought to have felt does not tally with what the little girl so plainly felt.

The sheltered life of the Martin household, and the extraordinary regard in which all her relatives held her, did not, on any except an academic level, prepare Thérèse very well for school. At eight and a half she was sent as a day-girl to the Abbey school,[23] where Léonie was a boarder and Céline already a day-girl. 'I've often heard it said that one's school-days are the best and the happiest days of one's life,' says Thérèse ruefully 'but I can't say I found them so . . . I was like some little flower that has always been accustomed to put out its frail roots in a soil specially prepared for it; such a flower does not take kindly to a garden which it shares with a variety of others, many of them hardier than itself, which also draw, from a common soil, the vitality it needs.'[24] The unconscious narcissism and snobbery of this remark does not detract from its truth. Thérèse's upbringing *had* made her into an exotic, a hothouse bloom, one very poorly adapted to holding its own in normal life.

Part of Thérèse's school problem was that she was much further advanced in school work than her contemporaries which meant that she was in a class with girls much bigger than herself. Then, she appeared to invite the spite of one of the girls in the class who teased her continually. Nothing in Thérèse's previous experience showed her any way to deal with this except to cry about it. Her cleverness, or her old-fashioned way of talking, seemed to put off her classmates, and she was unable to make a friend. If she had not been able to join Céline in the breaks from the classroom she thought that she would not have survived the humiliation of being always alone.

The irony was that in some ways she was a great success at school; she was doing very well in her lessons, and she loved going home, announcing her good marks to Papa and showing him the badge she had been given. Papa usually gave her a shining threepenny bit which she immediately put into a box she kept for charitable donations. Pauline, on the other hand, gave her a hoop, perfect for playing in the long alley outside Les Buissonets.

Thursday afternoons, as is usual in French schools, was a holiday, but Thérèse was dismayed to discover she was not allowed to spend it as she liked. She was obliged to play games 'not just with Céline . . . but with my Guérin cousins and the Maudelonde girls. I looked on it as a penance.'[25] Little Thérèse was becoming very precious indeed, though she does say that it must have been pretty boring for the other children having her around. The trouble was that she had forgotten how to behave like a child. Try as she would she no longer had the knack of it.

Other Thursday afternoons were spent dancing, usually quadrilles which she hated as much as she hated playing games. Just occasionally the children were taken to a local park instead, where Thérèse showed an unexpected skill in finding the prettiest flowers and picking them faster than anyone else.

Only once did Thérèse shine at playing which was when she hit on the idea of playing hermits. Several of the children pretended they lived in rude huts with a few vegetables and a small cornfield. They took it in turns to be 'active' or to pray, both parts of the hermit life being carried out in complete silence. So fascinated did she and Marie Guérin become by this play that when her aunt arrived to take them home they insisted on telling imaginary beads as they walked along the street, making ostentatious signs of the cross over the buns that they were given for tea.

One good thing that happened was that she and her cousin Marie became very close – twin souls, Thérèse says. There were, fortunately, a lot of jokes and some shared games, including the one where they walked along a crowded pavement keeping their eyes shut until they fell into an array of open boxes arranged outside a shop and got a telling-off from the shopkeeper.

The old affection for Céline did not diminish. Céline was much more robustly disobedient than Thérèse, and generally a much bolder child. When Thérèse was teased and bullied at school Céline stood up for her. Like the big girls, she seemed inordinately anxious over Thérèse's health. Céline's carefulness of

Thérèse was so great that the family called Thérèse 'Céline's little daughter'. Mothering Thérèse had become a general occupation for the Martin sisters.

When Céline was prepared for her First Communion by Marie, Thérèse listened carefully, longing to be eleven and have her turn. For three days before the great event, Céline went away to a retreat, and Thérèse was inconsolable at her absence.

A much worse loss was about to strike her. Pauline, at twenty-three, felt the call to a Carmelite vocation, and visits to the Carmel in Lisieux established that they would be prepared to accept her as a postulant. Thérèse overheard Pauline telling Marie about this decision.

It was a terrible way to learn such news, and it cut Thérèse to the heart. 'I was going to lose my mother all over again,' she says pitiably. 'I can't tell you what misery I went through at that moment; this was life . . . when you saw it as it really was [it] just meant continual suffering, continual separation.'[26] Apart from anything else she felt betrayed by Pauline. Playfully in the past, when Thérèse had announced her ambition to become an anchoress (a hermit who lived a solitary life enclosed in a cell), Pauline had said that they would go off and become anchoresses together one day. Unknown to her Thérèse had fantasised about this glorious future.

Now Thérèse, always prone to crying, wept uncontrollably. Pauline very gently took her on her knee and began to tell her about life in the Carmel. Thérèse, only nine, went away and brooded about it and came up with an extraordinary response. 'I came to the conclusion that this must be the desert in which God meant me, too, to take refuge. So strong was my feeling about this that it left no shadow of doubt in my mind; it wasn't just the dream of an impressionable child, it was certain with all the certainty of a divine vocation.'[27] It is true that from this time on Thérèse never wavered in her determination to become a Carmelite nun until she in fact became one.

The next day she told Pauline of this new development and Pauline, humouring her, said that she would take her to the Carmel to see Mother Marie de Gonzague, the Prioress, and

Thérèse could tell her the news of her vocation herself. A Sunday was fixed for the visit, though to Thérèse's annoyance her cousin Marie was invited to come too. Because they were still children they were to be allowed into the enclosure instead of kept outside the grille. Thérèse was concerned that, with her cousin there, she would have no chance to confide that she, no less than Pauline, had a vocation. Insisting that she had private matters to discuss with the Prioress, and rather touchingly believing that she would be accepted as a postulant along with Pauline, Thérèse went into the parlour with Reverend Mother and told her the great news.

Reverend Mother received the confidence calmly and then pointed out that she couldn't receive a nine-year-old into Carmel. Thérèse must wait until she was at least sixteen. Thérèse, who might have had all this made clear to her by her own family, was heartbroken, since she could not face losing Pauline.

There were still several weeks before her sister was due to enter Carmel during which time Thérèse, pathetically, stuck to her like a limpet, endlessly buying her cakes and sweets. On 2 October Pauline entered, as Thérèse poetically puts it, 'the day when Our Lord picked the first flower in this garden of his.' The whole family wept, as usual. Poor little Thérèse 'looked up at the clear sky, and wondered how the sun could shine so brightly when my own heart was plunged in sorrow'.[28]

As ill luck would have it 2 October was also the day she had to return to hated school. After school she went back to Carmel, and for the first time went through the pain of talking to Pauline through the grille. It was the beginning of a period of desperate unhappiness. Although members of the family went frequently for visits they always went as a group. Thérèse, who had been used to having Pauline to herself, now had just a few snatched minutes which she was usually too tearful to make use of. It seemed to her that Pauline ignored her in favour of others. 'Deep in my heart I felt: "Pauline is lost to me." '[29]

During that winter she got more and more depressed and began to suffer from continual headaches, sleeplessness and skin trouble. At Easter, Louis took Marie and Léonie to Paris, leaving the younger children with the Guérins. Sensing that something was very wrong with Thérèse, Uncle Isidore spent time alone with the little girl, talking gently of her dead mother and telling her of plans that she and Céline should have lots of treats that Easter holiday. After this Thérèse looked so worn out that her aunt put her to bed, but Thérèse was seized with a fit of trembling, and despite blankets and hotwater bottles she shook all night, and suffered hallucinations.

The next day the doctor was called who said, rather enigmatically, that it was 'a very serious complaint'. When the rest of the family returned from Paris, Marie came to the Guérins to nurse Thérèse. The child continued very ill until, dramatically, on the day of Pauline's clothing as a nun, she got up seemingly perfectly well. Once again she had the opportunity to be held in Pauline's arms, of hugging and kissing her and sitting on her lap. 'I did get the chance of seeing her, looking so lovely, in her wedding dress.'[30]

This brief episode over, Thérèse returned to Les Buissonets and immediately became as ill as ever, suffering from delirium, rambling in her speech, sometimes unable to open her eyes, sometimes frenzied in her movements. She could not bear Marie out of her sight, and when she left the room to take meals or sleep and Victoire took over, Thérèse began calling hysterically for 'Mama'. Léonie too tried to help but was rejected by Thérèse, though Céline was permitted, in words used later by Thérèse, to 'shut herself up for hours with a sister who to all appearances was a lunatic'.[31]

The Martin family, reflecting on this illness in later years, decided quite simply that it was a visitation from the devil, a revenge for the attack Pauline had launched on him by going into the Carmel. In fact it seems to bear all the marks of hysteria, not least the dramatic recovery that lasted a day. Thérèse, deeply disturbed and angry at her desertion by a series of mothers, yet unable freely to admit her rage against God for taking her Pauline, had no alternative to falling ill, an attention-getting device which had the whole family continually tending to her.

Thérèse, though she repeats the story of the devil, seems to have some doubt about it, and reports her worry at the time about whether she was *really* ill or whether she was 'playing the invalid'. It continued to worry her so much that, when she entered Carmel years later she asked her confessor whether he thought she had been shamming. She was comforted by his insistence that this could not be possible.

In the intervals of delirium Thérèse cut pictures out of card-board to send to Pauline, or made daisy and forget-me-not wreaths to place on the statue of the Virgin which stood in the bedroom. It was May, the month of Our Lady, and while the sun blazed outside and the flowers bloomed, Thérèse was doomed to stay in bed. Pauline sent her 'child' presents – an hour-glass, and a doll dressed as a Carmelite, a present which Uncle Isidore, with rare insight as to the cause of Thérèse's illness, regarded as unnecessarily tactless. Louis paid for Masses for Thérèse's recovery at the Church of Our Lady of Victories in Paris.

One Sunday morning, 13 May, and the feast of Pentecost, a strange incident happened. Marie, who had nursed Thérèse during most of her illness, went out into the garden, leaving Thérèse with Léonie who was reading by the window. Thérèse, as usual, began her cry of 'Mama, mama!' Eventually Marie came back.

I was quite conscious of her entering the room, but I couldn't recognise with any certainty who it was, so I went on calling for 'Mama' louder than ever. It was very painful to me, to have this unnatural conflict going on in my mind, and it must have been still more painful for Marie. When she found she couldn't convince me that she was really there, she knelt down beside my bed, with Léonie and Céline, turned towards Our Lady's statue and prayed for me like a mother praying for her child's life.[32]

Thérèse too turned towards the statue and prayed, asking for pity from 'her Mother in heaven'. Suddenly she had a vision of the Virgin smiling upon her and looking at her with infinite kindness. Thérèse burst into a flood of tears and from that moment her illness was over.

Chapter Four

A DROP LOST IN THE OCEAN

In the moment when she saw the Virgin smile Thérèse had found a mother who would not die or go away. The wound of her mother's death, reopened by Pauline's departure, was healed.

Although Thérèse began to resume normal life at once, a peculiarly painful circumstance surrounded the whole event. Without knowing quite what had happened Marie and the other two sisters realised that Thérèse had had some 'supernatural' experience, and Marie persisted in making her talk about it.

Thérèse was reluctant to do so. The experience had a feeling of extraordinary intimacy about it and like all such experiences, it was impossible to describe it accurately or even truthfully in words. But the child was accustomed to obeying her sisters and when Marie would not leave the subject alone she did her best to explain what had happened. At once she sensed that in some way she had spoiled, or betrayed, the trust and favour shown her by the Virgin and felt deep shame. That was bad enough, but then Marie, delighted with her description, passed the story on to Carmel and when Thérèse went there on a visit she found the convent was agog with it. There was no end to the questions. Was the Blessed Virgin carrying the infant Jesus in her arms, the nuns wanted to know. What did her face look like? Was she surrounded by light?

The questions muddled Thérèse who became unsure of what it was she had seen. Once again she wondered if she had made the whole thing up. The more they questioned her the more she contradicted herself, and the sillier and more miserable she began to feel. She knew, much too late, that she should have kept her vision to herself.

Her piety deepened. She had romantic fantasies of herself as a Carmelite and decided she would like to be called Thérèse of the Child Jesus, because of her special devotion to the divine child. She knew herself now as one marked out by God.

She still missed Pauline badly, although the old desperation was gone. She found one ingenious way to keep in touch with her. She took over her sister's old studio, an attic, and furnished it to her own taste, with odds and ends she found around the house. There was a picture of Pauline, some of her old drawings, a hanging basket of grasses and flowers, a big black crucifix, an aviary full of birds – canaries and linnets – to whom Thérèse was devoted, a bookcase full of her school-books upon which stood a statue of our Lady, with fresh flowers and candles. There were other holy statues, including one of St Joseph, and various pious knicknacks. On her 'desk' by the window – a table with a green cloth on it – stood an hour-glass, a watch-case, some flower vases and an inkstand. There were some chairs and a doll's cot which had been Pauline's. She also had a 'hanging garden' outside the window, pots and window-boxes full of the flowers she loved to grow. The room satisfied her taste for pretty things.

Maybe to take her out of herself a little, or at least to provide a little healthy convalescence, Louis took Thérèse back to Alençon for a stay during the school holidays. There she was made much of, and the pair of them were continually invited out by friends and neighbours. She says that she was 'entertained, petted and admired'. It is difficult to imagine that Alençon was a very sophisticated town or that the entertainment of a ten-year-old consisted of much more than picnics, rides, meals, and visits, but in writing about it Thérèse manages to make it sound more than a little decadent and her hosts intolerably worldly and frivolous when they were only trying to give the little girl a good time.

Whether Thérèse had the puritan reaction at the time or only when she came to write her story in the convent is not really clear. Perhaps she just needs the story to point up the superiority of Carmel. One of the troubles of choosing to live 'out of the world' as Thérèse was to do, is that it seems to encourage a ludicrously melodramatic view of 'the world' and its failings as a way of heightening the wisdom of the choice to leave it. What annoys Thérèse, in retrospect, about their friends at Alençon is that they 'had the knack of serving God and at the same time enjoying, to the full, the good things of earth', a trick Thérèse was never really to learn.

Soon, however, she was back home again, preparing for an event she had longed for – her First Communion. This was a great step in the life of Catholic children, a sign that they had become adults in the faith and were allowed to join in the most important rite of the Church. It was painful that Pauline could not be the one to prepare Thérèse for it, as she had prepared Céline, but Pauline did write her a special little treatise of preparation, prettily decorated with roses, violets, bluebells and daisies. There were spaces in which Thérèse had to write down 'sacrifices' and 'acts', so that when the notebook was returned to Pauline she would be able to observe her progress.

Meanwhile Marie took her on her knee every night and talked to her about what her future life would be like and what a consolation her religion would be. Marie was warm, and comforting, much less exacting than Pauline. Maybe she had learned a sense of balance from her own acute religious struggles. It was a time of great closeness between the two sisters – Thérèse says, simply and beautifully, 'the great generosity of her heart passed into mine.'

Marie had not at this time decided what her own future was to be, whether she would enter the Carmel like Pauline or perhaps marry; she had Pauline's gift for teaching. She told Thérèse that what mattered most was fidelity over little things, a remark important for her sister's future development.

Thérèse, all by herself, had begun to work out a process of mental prayer, climbing into a private little space between the wall and her bedcurtain, and dwelling slowly and deeply on thoughts of God and eternity. Neither Marie nor her teachers realised that this was what she was doing, and they continued to teach her vocal prayers to say.

In addition to Marie's preparation Thérèse was taught her catechism at school at which, as in most subjects, she was top of the class; success mattered desperately to her and she used to burst into tears if someone else briefly took the top place from her, to the dismay of Abbé Domin who took the class. In happier moments he called her his little Doctor which gave her tremendous pleasure. Her other gifts were for writing and history. She could also sometimes command the admiration of the other girls by being a good story-teller, something which her autobiography bears out. She was one who naturally saw life in dramatic colours . . .

She was still a strange, even morbid, child, picking up dead birds from the school grounds and burying them in a bird cemetery she had started. As before she made tentative overtures of friendship with other children and for a time thought that two of them really cared for her, but was dismayed to discover that her feelings were much more intense than theirs, and 'I wasn't prepared to go about asking for affection when there was no disposition to give it', she says tartly.

Céline had developed a crush on one of the mistresses, a 'special friendship' as Thérèse calls it, and her sentimental feelings were returned. Thérèse timidly tried to follow her example, but without success. Looking back on this she says that it was just as well that she had 'so little gift for making myself agreeable' since human love makes the love of God impossible. The trouble with human love, she goes on to surmise out of her narrow experience, is that to love a human being is inevitably to love 'immoderately'. Certainly she had loved Pauline 'immoderately' and it is not surprising that human love had come to seem dangerous to her.

In one of those melodramatic flights which reveal how little she knew of the world, she claims that if God had not cut her off from human relationships she might have 'fallen as low as St Mary Magdalen', a fate rather difficult for us to believe in. No doubt she imagines the life of the prostitute as one of unbridled

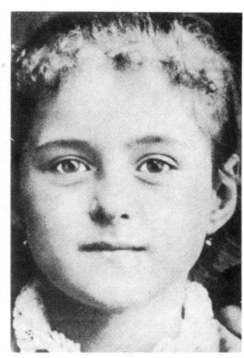

Thérèse as an eight-year-old

Thérèse aged three

Les Buissonnets

The interior of Les Buissonnets

Thérèse aged fifteen, with her hair up to impress the Bishop

Thérèse as a novice, aged sixteen

The Carmelite cloister and garden

The Carmelite Church

The refectory at Carmel

Thérèse's cell

Thérèse in 1894, the year she started to write her autobiography

Thérèse three months before her death

A typical statue of Thérèse in a village church

lust, a fate that no conceivable set of circumstances would have seemed likely to impose on Thérèse Martin. Yet she may be telling us something important about herself, that she perceives within her rather sad struggles to obtain human love – from schoolmates and a teacher – something insatiable that she knows in advance can never be satisfied. The repeated losses of her infancy and childhood have left her with a legacy of longing and fear so great that to live with love means to evoke the terrible danger of loss. The risk is intolerable. The love of God, though it lacks precisely 'the human touch', has the total advantage in that it can never be lost except perhaps by one's own wilful choice. Already, on the threshold of adolescence, she had decided that loving relationships outside her own family were too difficult and painful to be attempted. So far as we know she was only to deny this decision once.

Soon Thérèse, like Céline before her, went for her First Communion retreat at the Abbey, which meant becoming a boarder for a week. It was a rite of passage by which you passed from being a child to being one of the big girls. Now bigger and stronger – eleven years old – she felt much better able to cope with separation from the family than in the past. She loved being part of a religious community for a few days and rather ostentatiously wore a huge cross when she attended the offices. The mistresses and girls were rather startled to find that she did not know how to dress herself without help, nor to comb her own hair and she had to be helped out by a kind teacher. It poses the question 'Did the Martin sisters need Thérèse to remain as a baby, or maybe a live dolly whom they dressed and cared for?' It suggests that she had become very passive, letting the control of her life and of herself pass entirely into the hands of her sisters.

Predictably, she enjoyed the retreat tremendously. She had daily visits from Papa, Marie and Léonie, she listened with enormous pleasure to the addresses, and worked hard at her meditations. She made her confession on the eve of her Communion and received absolution, and then on the great day itself, 8 May, she and the other girls put on their dresses 'white as snowflakes'. It was the happiest day of her life, so happy that she could not stop crying, something which baffled her fellow-Communicants. She was selected to say a prayer of consecration on behalf of all the other children.

By an odd chance it was also the day of Pauline's Profession (the taking of life-vows), and that evening Louis took Thérèse, dressed in the lovely dress that Marie had made her, to Carmel where she saw Pauline wearing the crown of roses. Papa gave Thérèse a watch as a present.

First Communion had been a much more profound experience than her relatives guessed, or than many of her schoolmates can have known themselves. It seemed to her that the 'first kiss of the Lord [was] imprinted on my soul! A lover's kiss; I knew that I was loved, and I, in my turn, told him that I loved him, and was giving myself to him for all eternity.' It also seemed to her that 'Thérèse had simply disappeared, like a drop lost in the ocean'.[33]

Alongside this act of self-surrender Thérèse's long fascination with suffering had become manifest. Talking with her about her spiritual life, as Marie frequently did, Marie said to her one day that suffering was a path that she probably would not have to tread, that she 'would always be carried like a little child in the arms of God's mercy'. Almost at once Thérèse felt a great attraction to suffering. She had already entered the strange tortured world of Thomas à Kempis and at Communion used to repeat the words from the *Imitation*, 'Jesus, sweet to the taste beyond all our telling, turn all earthly consolations into bitterness for me.'[34] Marie had little idea of Thérèse's new ambition.

A lonely little girl who cannot find acceptance among her peers, who has endured repeated experiences of bereavement, who has been encouraged in a scrupulous and perhaps morbid environment, already knows a lot about suffering. Suddenly a new path offers itself which seems to offer a degree of control lacking before. If suffering is embraced instead of avoided some of the sting is taken out of it. If it is also true, as Pauline had seemed to suggest to her, that it has positive usefulness in bringing God's love to others by actually bearing the pain in their place (what is called substitutive suffering), in itself an imitation of Jesus bearing the sin and suffering of the world upon the cross, then she can find glory in her ignominious pain, though it is necessarily a somewhat secret glory. She has found a pathway through the insoluble problem of being helpless Thérèse, though it is a tragic one.

Her spirits were cheered by her Confirmation and by picking enormous quantities of marguerites for Corpus Christi. 'Dear little Léonie stood godmother' to her at her Confirmation. Léonie was twenty-one, and the adjectives seem contemptuous.

At school Thérèse found her schoolfellows more 'worldly' than ever and they found her still more insufferable. They believed her impossibly spoilt by her family – noting the gifts Louis lavished on the little queen and the way he insisted, amusingly in view of the family ideas about modesty, that her hair must be freshly curled every night.

The annual retreat brought a problem that had been threatening for many a year – scruples. 'My lightest thoughts, my simplest actions, troubled my conscience afterwards.'[35] She would report these torturing thoughts to Marie, obtain reassurance from her, only to feel the excruciating pangs of guilt return. The misery of 'scruples' coincided, not altogether surprisingly, with the onset of adolescence.

Meanwhile Céline, now sixteen, had finished her schooling at the Abbey and left. Unable to continue without the support of her sister, Thérèse broke down, with continual blinding headaches, and Louis, by now thoroughly anxious about her health, allowed her to leave school too. Instead of school, she took lessons at the house of a widow, Madame Papinau. Madame Papinau's mother lived with her, and received a string of visitors, many of whom made complimentary remarks about the prettiness of the teenage girl and the beauty of her fair hair. With her usual ambivalence Thérèse tells us both how much people admired her and how this would have made her vain if God had not snatched her away from the world in time.

No doubt Thérèse's shaky self-esteem needed a boost, but

perhaps we may wonder whether she was quite as pretty as she would later have liked to believe. (If you are going to renounce the pleasures of your youth and beauty for Jesus the better the looks the greater the renunciation. If you are plain, it suggests you have only embraced Jesus *faute de mieux*.)

How attractive was Thérèse at this stage of her life? Photographs of Thérèse in her teens show her as vivacious and attractive, with bright eyes, but with over-full cheeks and the small mouth that seemed peculiar to the Martin sisters.

Leaving the Abbey school before she had finished her education created a special problem for Thérèse. The school, like many Catholic schools, had a special pious society the girls were allowed to join called the Association of the Holy Angels. In their mid-teens, if they were known for leading devout lives, they were allowed to join a club for older girls called The Children of Mary. Thérèse very much wanted to join this. Leaving the Abbey school, however, made her no longer eligible. She braved the headmistress who, obviously piqued by her leaving early, said that she would decide whether Thérèse was a suitable candidate if, for the time being, she spent two afternoons a week at the Abbey. So, twice a week, Thérèse drifted in and out of classes, ignored by everybody, until she finished up praying in front of the Blessed Sacrament until Papa arrived to take her home. 'Our Lord was my only real Friend, the only Person I could really talk to.' Then, with a touch of sour grapes she adds 'What more could I want?'[36]

But the bitter loneliness of her schooldays still haunted her. She wandered about the Abbey feeling, as she says 'depressed and ill', punished by nuns and girls alike for evading a school life that had become intolerable. Once again she began to yearn for eternity.

The Guérins took Thérèse and Céline to the seaside and did their best to give them a lighthearted holiday at Trouville where they stayed at the Chalet des Lilas. They rode on donkeys and went paddling and shrimping. Aunt Céline gave Thérèse some pretty blue hair ribbon, which thrilled her until scruples set in and she felt obliged to go to confession about it.

Marie Guérin was going through a hypochondriacal fit, continually crying and complaining of headaches. Marie was a pretty child, if anything more spoiled than Thérèse, and her aunt made an endless fuss of her. Thérèse, who suffered quite a lot from headaches herself, decided to copy Marie's attention-getting methods, but found to her dismay that nobody believed her headaches were the problem and that they started probing for some deeper cause for her malaise. Ashamed of herself and humiliated at her cry for love and attention she decided that, for reasons mysterious to her except in terms of the will of God, she was not intended to be cherished in that sort of way.

A further blow was about to fall on her – her sister Marie's decision to enter Carmel. Marie had never had Pauline's clear sense of vocation, and she only made the decision now because her confessor told her that it was what God wanted her to do. Thérèse had given up her dependency on Pauline with the greatest difficulty and only because she really had no alternative. 'It had been terrible', she says, 'trying to get accustomed to living without her, but there was a barrier between us you couldn't cross, and you had to admit it, Pauline was lost to me as if she'd been dead.'[37] For Thérèse her relationship with her big sisters was partly a matter of physical contact – sitting on their knees, even as a big girl, embracing them or having her hair done – partly a matter of long, luxurious conversations in which she confided all her feelings. Carmel, with its grille and its supervised conversations, made such relationships impossible, at great cost to Thérèse.

She had lost Pauline, her beloved 'petite mère' in this fashion and now, she was told, she was to lose Marie. Her immediate response was reminiscent of her behaviour when Pauline prepared to leave. She followed Marie about, continually knocked at her door and covered her with kisses, and burst into tears at the least provocation. Louis, with a wan hope of distraction, took her to Alençon, but there she broke down and wept hopelessly at Zélie's grave, distraught, it seemed, simply because she had forgotten to bring the flowers she had picked specially. Remembering the occasion years later, when she no longer broke down nor needed anyone, she also remembered the sting of what people in Alençon had said about her. 'A weak character.' Emotional adolescent girls were nothing unusual, but the youngest Martin girl seemed to be continually in tears as well as being too pious for her own good.

Piety was in the air that summer. Léonie, perhaps not wanting to be outdone by Marie, desperate to carve a niche for herself in a family where only piety counted, went off to the Poor Clares in Lisieux while the family were on holiday in Alençon and got herself accepted as a postulant without telling anybody. Perhaps it was an unspoken rebuke to her sisters for the method of their melodramatic departures from 'the world'. It certainly has the feeling of a dash for freedom and a longing to count in a family where she seemed scarcely to exist. Significantly, her going did not seem to trouble Thérèse very much in itself, though she was hurt that Léonie was prepared to go without saying goodbye, and, like all the Martins, she thought it 'very odd'. Louis, and the three girls at home, found it somehow embarrassing. They all went to see Léonie in her new habit, who said that they must be sure of taking a good look at her eyes – after this she would always have to lower them in public.

Alas for Léonie's bid for escape, after two months she was back home again not having made a success of life as a Poor Clare. 'We saw those blue eyes of hers again', Thérèse tells us, 'often wet with tears.'[38]

On 15 October Marie joined Pauline at the Carmel, and the usual heartbreaking ritual was enacted once again. The first effect of losing yet another deeply-loved person was a recurrence of Thérèse's torturing scruples. This time there was no one to turn to. On an inspiration Thérèse prayed to her brothers and the sister who had died in infancy asking them to intercede for her, 'reminding them that I'd always been the darling, the spoilt child of the family, because I was the youngest, and if they'd lived they'd have been as kind to me as the rest.'[39]

As if trying to grow up Thérèse now began to do a few – a very few – household chores. Just before her fourteenth birthday there was to be another milestone in her growing up. On

Christmas Eve the Martin children, like other French children, placed their boots in the chimney corner, and returned from Midnight Mass to find them filled with sweets and little presents. Devoted to family rituals and still very much a little girl, Thérèse loved this treat and looked forward to it. Dashing upstairs to take off their hats before starting on the delights of their 'boots' Thérèse and Céline overheard Louis say, 'Well! thank goodness, it's the last year we shall have to do this!' Depressed, beset with strong-minded daughters who went their own way, Louis had had a difficult year.

Thérèse was stricken by the coldness of this, as Céline saw at once. 'Don't go down yet,' Céline advised, 'it'll only make you miserable.' But in a gesture that felt of great importance to Thérèse, a moment of self-victory, she dried her tears, and went downstairs, smiling, to unpack the boots with every appearance of unalloyed pleasure. It is a story which opens a window on a strange world, one in which self-conquest mattered more than truthfulness in relationship (why *should* Louis be deceived in this way?). But the incident gave Thérèse a new sense of strength – it was, she says, as if she'd recovered the self she lost at four and a half when her mother died.

Another reassuring thing happened. Thérèse had become very interested in stories of a criminal called Pranzini who had murdered two women and a child in the course of committing a robbery; she prayed diligently for his repentance and arranged to have a Mass said for him. Then she asked Our Lord for a sign that her efforts for Pranzini had been rewarded. Sure enough, as she discovered when she broke Papa's injunction against reading newspapers and followed up the story of the execution, she learned that Pranzini, about to lay his head on the block beneath the guillotine, had wept and kissed a crucifix three times. The knowledge of Pranzini's repentance was very important to Thérèse. Through it, she had discovered, as it were, a vocation within a vocation.

Thérèse's formal education was now over. She was fourteen and she now had little to do except pray and read, both of which she did a great deal. She knew the *Imitation* so thoroughly that her aunt used to tease her by opening it at random, giving her a line or two's prompt, and then letting her recite it from memory from there. In the summer she carried it always in her pocket; in winter in her muff. Céline had, in some measure, become her confidante now, and they sat up late at night talking of their aspirations – the incident over the 'souliers' at Christmas had brought them very close.

When she was little Thérèse had longed for Céline to confide in her and Céline, in the cruel manner of children, had refused to do so, saying that she was a 'baby'. Now Thérèse had suddenly grown tall, and seemed so much more mature that it seemed as if the two girls were the same age, or even perhaps that Thérèse had overtaken Céline and become the leader.

The fact that soon became very clear to both of them was that Thérèse was simply filling in time until she was received into Carmel. She had no other ambition than this, no thought of marriage or of 'having a good time', no real duties or interests. Not surprisingly, her rather scheming character began to revolve plots as to how this cherished plan could be achieved.

There was a formidable line-up of obstacles. The first of them was her age – sixteen was the minimum age, and a wait of eighteen months seemed out of the question to her. Marie, who probably understood Thérèse better than anyone, said simply that she was too young. Pauline, on the other hand, subtly encouraged her, and Céline found the whole idea too thrillingly heroic for words and was her sister's staunch ally.

Thérèse knew, all along, that the worst person to tell would be Papa, since to lose his 'little queen' would cost him far more than losing Pauline and Marie to Carmel. While the two girls were plotting, Louis, who may well have understood more than they imagined, had a stroke which left him temporarily paralysed. He recovered from the worst of it fairly quickly, suffering only a weakness of the legs and the depression which was more or less habitual to him. One of the oddest features of the Martin story, though, is that within less than a month of the stroke, Thérèse, well knowing how Louis doted on her, informed him of her wish to enter Carmel at fifteen and asked for his permission.

Did she fear to see her father die, as her mother had done, or worry that he was about to become an invalid, so that she would be stuck with the role of sick-nurse and would have to postpone her entry to Carmel indefinitely? Only the sense that she needed to get away for her very survival would seem to justify the apparent cruelty of informing a sick man that he was about to lose the person he loved most on earth for reasons of no greater urgency than Pauline's abrupt departure when Thérèse had badly needed her.

On the feast of Pentecost, 29 May, at sunset, when Louis was sitting in the garden by the well, Thérèse went and sat beside him, and told him of her ambition. He wept as she told him of her desire to enter Carmel, but said no word to discourage her except to suggest that she was very young. They walked up and down the garden while he tried to take in the enormity of it, tried to say that God was doing him an immense honour in taking one daughter after another.

At one point he pulled some tiny white lilies from a wall and gave them to Thérèse as a sort of analogy of her own life. She noticed that he had plucked the flower, root and all, and thought that, like it, her roots were about to be transplanted. She pressed the little plant between the leaves of the *Imitation*, and there it remained 'only the stalk has broken off now, close to the roots, as if God meant to tell me that he's going to sever my connection with this earth before long.'[40]

Chapter Five

A TOY OF NO VALUE

After Marie's departure Céline and Thérèse had enjoyed a liberty unusual for young women in the nineteenth century. Louis was too depressed and too lost in otherworldly pursuits to play the interfering parent, and in any case Thérèse's wish was his command. Léonie, in another attempt at the religious life, had entered the convent of the Visitation at Caen. In marked contrast to her distress at the loss of her other sisters Thérèse does not even mention it in her writing. With all three of the big sisters out of the way, Céline and Thérèse could do as they liked.

Some teenage girls might have used this opportunity to chase boys, to take up artistic pursuits (the sisters did, in fact, attempt a little drawing), or to fall into romantic daydreams, but the Martin girls were single-mindedly set on the religious life – this *was* their romance. Or at least it was Thérèse's.

Suddenly all her immense energy and determination became constellated around this single aim, and all the people who might have been considered her natural allies became foes, or anyhow opponents to be won round. Uncle Isidore was one of them. Regarded as the head of the Guérin/Martin clan and in some ways more of a father to Thérèse than Louis because less infatuated and more perceptive, he was plainly horrified when she told him of her ambition to become a Carmelite and flatly refused his permission. What was more he told her that she was not to raise the issue again until she was at least seventeen. He said it nicely, but he also pointed out, correctly, that she had no experience of the world, and that it would be 'the height of imprudence' for her to be admitted so young.

Thérèse's immediate response to this rebuff was to go into a three-day depression which she compared, excessively, to the agony of Jesus in the garden. It poured with rain for the whole three days, about which Thérèse remarked naively that she had often found that at critical moments in her life the weather behaved in appropriate fashion. For the rest of her life she had the annoying habit of speaking as if the weather was somehow attendant on her moods and private catastrophes.

On the fourth day she went back to see Uncle Isidore; sensing that he was beaten he wearily remarked that she was a flower God had decided to pick while it was in bud. He, like her aunt, was plainly distressed by her decision, but Thérèse cared little for that. She had won, and 'light of heart', as she said, she made her way home; the rain had ceased.

If Thérèse was untouched by the grief of her uncle and aunt she was still more oblivious to the pain of her father, who became more irritable and emotional than before. The pain of losing the child he had loved more than anyone, almost certainly including his wife (it was, after all, Thérèse, not Zélie, who was the 'queen') had begun to destroy him, but as in the case of Thérèse, when Pauline had left home, he could not argue with God, and the inner rage had to be ruthlessly suppressed. Determinedly oblivious that her actions might be relevant to her father's suffering, as Pauline had once been determinedly oblivious of hers, a few years later she was to write with a wonderful egotism of this time, 'It's a time of great suffering, but I feel that I've got the strength to bear worse trials than this.'

Louis's frailty did not prevent Thérèse pressing him into service when she took the next step on the road to achieving her object and went to see the Father Superior of the male Carmelite house whom the Bishop of Bayeux, Monsignor Hugonin, had delegated to attend to her request. He was cold and silently disapproving. Despite Louis strongly supporting Thérèse's appeal, as he would have supported almost anything she asked him to do, Father said that he could see no reason for hurry. If the child wanted to lead a Carmelite life she could start by

practising at home. If the Bishop personally took her part of
course he would not oppose him, but really he didn't feel. . . .

Thérèse burst into floods of tears, and father and daughter
left; it was pouring with rain. Louis, desperate at her distress,
offered to accompany her on a visit to the Bishop himself, and
Thérèse replied that she 'was so determined to carry my point
that I'd go to the Holy Father if the Bishop wouldn't let me
enter Carmel at fifteen'.

Some respite from these endeavours was gained by an act of
charity. Thérèse and Céline offered to take temporary care of
two little girls whose mother was dying. Thérèse talked so
glowingly to them of the Child Jesus that the elder child, aged
six, was much impressed. It struck Thérèse how easy it was to
influence children. Like Pauline before her, it seemed to her
that children were 'like wax to receive impressions for better or
worse', and like Pauline again, she had no uncertainties, or
hesitations, about what those impressions should be. What one
ought to do was 'train them from the very start'.

Soon, however, it was time for Louis and Thérèse to keep
their appointment with the Bishop of Bayeux. Thérèse put her
hair up for the occasion, and wore a pretty dress, in order to
seem as old as possible; the photograph of her taken for the
occasion has a faintly mischievous quality. Despite all the tears
and dramatics occasionally one suspects that Thérèse found the
process of getting herself into Carmel something of a lark.

The visit to Bayeux was not much fun, however. It was
obligingly pouring with rain yet again, and the father and
daughter went into Bayeux on the omnibus and had lunch at a
grand hotel to fortify themselves for the ordeal ahead. (The
special meal was Louis's idea, of course. Never very interested
in food, Thérèse did not do justice to the lunch, but she could
see Papa was trying his very best.)

They were still much too early for their appointment, and the
rain was still lashing down, so they hung about the Cathedral,
getting themselves embarrassingly mixed up with a funeral
party, though Thérèse said some lengthy prayers in an empty
chapel.

She was desperately nervous, realising that she had to give a good account of herself to get her own way. Louis, who could not imagine anyone refusing her anything, said that the Bishop was bound to give way. He was all set to send a telegram to Carmel the minute the meeting was over. M. Reverony, the clergyman they had been told to ask for, swept them up, asked her a few questions, and seeing the unshed tears beginning to gather in her eyes said, 'Now then, no diamonds, please. His Lordship wouldn't like it.' Thereupon they were whisked through several vast rooms into a study with a blazing fire and three large armchairs.

Louis and Thérèse knelt to receive the Bishop's blessing, the Bishop and Louis took the two chairs by the fireplace and Thérèse, with some difficulty, was persuaded to take the seat in the middle.

Giving her reasons was just as difficult as she had feared. As her shy observations fell one by one into the silence she could see that Mgr Hugonin was not impressed at all.

'Had she wanted to be a Carmelite for a long time?' he enquired at last.

'Oh yes,' she replied from the vantage point of her fifteen years, 'a long, long time.' She went on to explain how ever since the age of reason she had planned to be a nun, and that more lately Carmel had seemed just the right place to fulfil her longing.

'What about her father?' the Bishop asked. 'Should she not stay and be a comfort to him for a few years yet?' Louis loyally interrupted at this point to say that *of course* Thérèse must be allowed to go into Carmel if that was what she wanted. Thérèse thought the Bishop must be very surprised and impressed by this.

The Bishop stalled by saying that he would have to talk some more with the Father Superior, and remembering how disapproving of her he had seemed Thérèse broke the interdict on tears and cried freely. This softened the Bishop, who put a comforting arm round her, at which she leant her head on his shoulder and sobbed uncontrollably. When he had had enough of this he saw them out into the garden, and Louis told him artlessly about Thérèse having put her hair up specially. Perhaps he thought it would make him realise the strength of her resolution. Thérèse, not surprisingly, cried all the way home. Only a visit to Pauline at Carmel comforted her.

Desperate to lighten the atmosphere, Louis had prepared a tremendous treat for her, though like all his treats, it was rather damply received. Maybe with some intention of distracting her, either temporarily or permanently, or maybe just because he had always liked travelling, he proposed to take Céline and Thérèse for a grand tour of Europe. Knowing very well that no holiday would succeed with Thérèse if presented simply as fun, he chose a pilgrimage which would include a visit to Rome and an audience with the Pope in the itinerary. A number of people from Lisieux were going and as it turned out M. Reverony was of the company.

The pilgrimage began in Paris, but Louis took the two girls there a few days beforehand so that they could see the sights. He was, for once, in tremendous spirits, humming old tunes to himself, and showing off his favourite places. Thérèse only really came to life in the church of Our Lady of Victories, a place she had wanted to see ever since her miracle cure. The pilgrims set off from Montmartre, offering their intention to God at Sacré Coeur. Thérèse, who had been shy at first of the society ladies and priests who were fellow-pilgrims began to be more sociable. She noticed M. Reverony's eye on her several times, and thought he was watching to see whether she would make a good Carmelite.

She was tremendously excited as the train passed through the Swiss countryside, rushing from one side of the railway carriage to the other, gasping at the beauty of the mountains. The combination of majesty and prettiness in the little villages appealed to her enormously. 'That God should have seen fit to squander such masterpieces on a world of exile!' she exclaimed rather pompously. In fact, the splendour of the landscape may have threatened her resolve to become a Carmelite in a way that made her very uncomfortable. The thought that it might be a great pity to give up such a beautiful world, and that there might not even be a very good reason for doing so, was ruthlessly suppressed. She dealt with the overwhelming experience of natural beauty by promising herself that when she was 'shut up' she would use these sights to recall the greatness and power of God. 'No attraction for me about the puppet-shows of earth, now that I've had this foretaste of what our Lord has in store for those who love him.' The priggishness of this is somehow pathetic.

When they got to Milan Thérèse and Céline proved themselves indefatigable sightseers, inspecting every statue in the cathedral, dogging the Bishop's footsteps as he showed the relics, climbing the marble towers, examining the Campo Santo grave by grave.

Then there was Venice, Padua and Bologna, which was quite spoiled for Thérèse because a forward university student lifted her down from the train to the platform. Eventually the train drew into Rome and the sleeping travellers were woken by the porters shouting 'Roma, Roma'.

They 'did' all the sights. Predictably for Thérèse and Céline the high spot was the Colosseum – 'the arena in which so many martyrs had shed their blood for Christ – at last I should be able to kneel and kiss that holy ground.' But a cruel disappointment was in store for her. The arena turned out to be a litter of fallen masonry which visitors were expected to contemplate from behind a distant barrier. There, far below, was the special bit of paving on which so many martyrs had suffered, and Thérèse could barely see it. She looked vainly round for a ladder, and seeing no other hope for it, climbed over the barrier, shouting to Céline to do the same and started plunging down into the ruins, the ground crumbling beneath her at every step.

Louis and the guide were at first too thunderstruck to make any sound. Then Louis started feebly issuing orders to them to return, orders Thérèse, with her usual wilfulness, had not the slightest intention of obeying. Bruised and filthy, the two girls reached the bit of pavement, sank on their knees before it, and kissed the dust of the place where the martyrs had died. 'I asked for the grace to bear a martyr's witness to our Lord,' says

Thérèse, 'and felt deep in my heart that the prayer had been granted.'

The two girls snatched up a stone or two and returned by the perilous way they had come. It was naughty, but undeniably brave. In the Catacombs too they filched some earth from St Cecilia's church, and in the Church of St Agnes Thérèse worked loose a little red stone in the mosaic to present to the saint's namesake, Pauline, Sister Agnes, on her return. The two girls were high on the excitement and the fervid emotion of the pilgrimage.

The high spot of the tour was, of course, the audience with Pope Leo XIII. Frantic with nervousness they put on their black dresses, their lace mantillas, and the papal medal with its blue and white ribbon, and set off for the Pope's chapel in the Vatican. After Mass the Pope sat down in an armchair and the pilgrims approached one by one, kissing first his foot, then his hand, and finally receiving his benediction. Then the members of the papal guard touched each kneeling pilgrim on the shoulder and it was time to get up and make way for the next pilgrim.

Thérèse and Céline, like the naughty self-willed girls they were, had hatched a rather bold plan. When it was time for Thérèse to kneel down, instead of crouching dumbly there, she would speak up and ask the Pope's permission to enter Carmel early. It had been one thing to think this idea up in an hotel room; it was a resolve that became terrifying as her turn in the line approaching the Holy Father grew nearer. A number of priests stood round the Papal chair, among them M. Reverony. With shrewd insight into the girl with whom he had to deal M. Reverony remarked to the pilgrims in general that they must not speak to the Pope since there was not enough time.

Alarmed by this, perhaps wanting to give up her wild resolve, Thérèse turned anxiously to Céline, who immediately said 'Speak out!' With the air of one brave enough to dare all for the cause Thérèse kissed the Pope's foot, and then clasped her hands together, tears swimming into her eyes, and informed the Holy Father that she had a favour to ask of him. 'Most Holy

Father,' she went on while Pope Leo's great dark eyes stared into hers, 'in honour of your jubilee, I want you to let me enter the Carmelite order at fifteen.'

The Pope seemed stunned by this approach and turned questioningly to M. Reverony, who explained that Thérèse was known to him, that she wanted to enter Carmel, and that the case was being looked into.

'Very well, my child,' said the Pope, 'do what your superiors tell you.'

This wouldn't do for Thérèse at all, so she clutched the Pope's knees and continued, 'Yes, but if you'd say the word, Most Holy Father, everybody would agree.'[41]

To which the Pope replied slowly and with conviction, 'All's well, all's well; if God wants you to enter, you will.'

Thérèse was just about to start debating this with him, and Céline was also chipping in to vouch for the strength of Thérèse's vocation when the Papal guards, helped by M. Reverony, lifted her bodily to her feet. 'I kept my arms on the Pope's knees,' says Thérèse without shame, 'and they had to carry me away by main force.'[42] They carried her to the exit where she and Céline and Louis were soon reunited, the two girls in tears, and Louis as usual more upset at Thérèse's distress than at her bad behaviour. The skies of Rome had clouded over for the occasion.

Describing this in her autobiography Thérèse begins to expound her fantasy of herself as an idle plaything of the Child Jesus, a 'toy of no value', say a ball. 'He can throw it on the ground, kick it about, make a hole in it, leave it lying in a corner, or press it to his heart if he feels that way about it.'[43] In Rome, she fantasised, he made a hole in the ball to see what was inside it, and then abandoned it.

The grand tour continued with visits to Pompeii and Naples, Assisi, Florence, Pisa and Genoa, with the Martins always staying at the best hotels and seeing marvellous scenery. Thérèse says, with adolescent grandiosity, that there was no balm for a bruised heart in gilded ceilings, marble staircases and silk hangings. All she wanted to make her happy was Carmel. In

Florence she touched one of the nails used in the crucifixion.

She returned to Lisieux at the beginning of December, half expecting, for no very good reason, that she would be safely inside Carmel by Christmas. She went to the Carmel as soon as they returned to Lisieux, to take the little piece of filched mosaic to Pauline and to pour out all her adventures. Pauline was sympathetic as usual, and suggested another letter to the Bishop. Christmas came without further sign, though Thérèse had haunted the post office for days for the Bishop's reply.

On her return from Midnight Mass, the time when once Thérèse had looked so eagerly at the contents of the 'souliers', Thérèse found a bowl in which Céline had arranged a floating ship. The name of the ship was 'Self-Abandonment'. On this tiny ship the Child Jesus lay asleep with a ball close beside him.

Despite Céline's love Thérèse wept her way through Christmas Day till afternoon came and it was time to go off and visit Pauline at Carmel. The Carmelites, by now fully aware of the drama Thérèse had created around herself, had prepared a gift for her – a statue of the Child Jesus holding a ball in his hand with the name of Thérèse written upon it. Thérèse's fantasy of being a plaything of Jesus, perhaps confided to Pauline, had taken the fancy of the nuns. When she had got over this surprise the nuns sang a hymn about Jesus written specially by Pauline.

New Year's Day brought a mixed blessing. She learned that the Bishop had given his consent to her entry to Carmel, but that Carmel itself in the person of the Prioress, Mother Marie de Gonzague, had decided to postpone admitting her until Easter. It seems likely that they did this to spare the postulant the rigours of Lent and of winter cold right at the beginning of her time in the religious life, but Thérèse, with her usual fierce determination to have things her way, raged and wept about it, almost as if they had rejected her altogether. How could she possibly wait so long – a whole three months?

In the end she reconciled herself to the disappointment by devising small acts of renunciation and discipline for herself: 'to repress the rejoinder which sometimes came to my lips; to do little acts of kindness without attracting any attention to them;

to sit upright instead of leaning back in my chair.'[44] She seemed to feel this would make her 'less unworthy of a heavenly Bridegroom'. Once she had discovered that, rail as she might, nothing was going to get her into Carmel before Easter, she settled down to using this last three months 'in the world' as well as she could.

Chapter Six

THE LITTLE BRIDE

On the Feast of the Annunciation, 9 April 1888, Thérèse at last entered Carmel. She had found her way into one of the most austere of the religious orders. The Carmelite Order, for men, was founded in Palestine by St Berthold around 1154. By 1250 a 'Rule', a system of practice, had been laid down of extreme asceticism. In 1452 an Order of Carmelite Sisters was founded. In the earliest centuries of the Church, before there were religious orders, there had been many who had chosen, as individuals, to live as hermits in deserts and caves, giving up their lives to the contemplation of God. For some this had been a wonderfully fruitful experience. Others had lost themselves in loneliness and madness, and it was in an attempt to provide a more structured life in which to worship God that founders like St Benedict in the sixth century had collected communities together and drawn up sets of guidelines – Rules – to govern their behaviour.

The Benedictines were not primarily interested in solitude, but in a life of communal prayer, study, and manual work. The Carmelites attempted something different, a system which provided a kind of communal solitude. Living together mainly in silence, groups of friars or of nuns devoted their time to reciting a cycle of prayers, usually composed of fragments of scripture (the Office), to performing the manual duties of the house, and to private 'mental prayer' (as opposed to 'vocal' or spoken prayer). Carmelite friars undertook preaching, hearing confessions, and the giving of retreats, occupations which gave them contact with the outside world. The nuns never left their houses, not even for such events as family funerals, and their contact with the outside world was extremely limited, usually to fairly brief conversations through an iron grating – 'the grille' – a system not unlike some kinds of prison visiting.

The Carmelite Order, the Order of Our Lady of Mount Carmel, had an eventful history. By the sixteenth century, the period of the Counter Reformation, its austerities had become relaxed and the way of life easy-going. The great Teresa (little Thérèse's namesake as Louis Martin had often pointed out), entering a convent in Avila as a young girl, found that it was a sort of gossip-shop for the town, with young men coming regularly to sit in the parlour to chat with the prettiest nuns. There were outings and visits to friends' houses, and a very leisurely programme of prayer. The atmosphere was rather like that of a high-class girls' boarding school.

Teresa, though naturally sociable, soon felt dissatisfied with a life that had neither the freedom of 'the world' nor any real devotion to prayer. As her own mystical genius flowered she set about reforming the Carmelite houses, travelling all over Spain to set up houses with a very different attitude to life and prayer. The reform was extensive, covering every detail of the life of a nun or friar.

Teresa restored the Office, the great twenty-four-hour cycle of prayer. Unlike, say the Cistercians, the Carmelites did not rise in the night and then go back to bed, but began their office at five, and then went on to an hour's mental prayer which in turn led up to the conventual Mass. This was spoken on ordinary days, sung upon Sundays and Feast days. After breakfast there was work until mid-morning when Sext and None were recited. Dinner followed and after dinner recreation, a period in which all sat together and talked – in the case of nuns they usually sewed or drew at the same time. Then Vespers, more work, another hour of mental prayer, supper, a short recreation, Compline, and bed.

Teresa worked out exactly what the reformed Carmelites should eat: they should have no meat, they should have no milk or eggs on fast days or on Fridays, they should fast from Holy

Cross Day, 14 September until Easter. They should have no linen but their blankets, sheets and underclothing should be of wool, and they should lie on a straw palliasse. Winter and summer, instead of shoes or boots, they should wear a pair of straw Spanish sandals known as alpargatas – it was this latter detail that gave the Reformed Carmelites the nickname of Discalced Carmelites, meaning 'Carmelites without shoes'. The houses were without heating in winter except in one room where the Carmelites might go for brief periods to warm themselves.

Unlike the nuns in the easy-going convent of Teresa's youth the Discalced were bent on finding out their own and each other's frailties and doing penance for them. In the daily Chapter of Faults they 'proclaimed' themselves and one another, and performed penances, often of a fairly humiliating kind. To be 'mortified' was thought to be good for one's own soul and for the souls of others – it was a sort of death in life that reminded you that you were dust. When rebuked by your superior you prostrated yourself and kissed the floor in a sort of gratitude.

The Rule of the Discalced was drawn up by Teresa not with an air of misery but with a passionate enthusiasm for the cause, an enthusiasm congruent with the Carmelite device 'Zelo zelatus sum pro Domino Deo exercituum' (With zeal have I been zealous for the Lord God of Hosts). It was a call to a life of heroism, a call often answered by those who otherwise might have had little opportunity to be heroes or heroines. Suffering otherwise endured by the poor because they had no alternative was chosen readily by men and women often of upper- or middle-class backgrounds as a sign of their devotion to God. It was part of the paradox of Christianity, the way it turned the standards of the world upside down, so that things there thought good (riches, material possessions) became meaningless in the light of eternity, and that things there thought bad (pain, hunger, discomfort, cold) were transformed by faith into joyful obedience.

What the Carmelite life was about, according to Teresa of Avila, was, first, the contemplation of God. It was for this freedom that women and men detached themselves from the life of the family and commerce. Having herself charted the degrees and modes of prayer with an almost clinical accuracy, Teresa set up a system whereby men and women, not necessarily as gifted as herself, had space and time for exploring the relationship with God.

Out of that relationship sprang other religious practices and forms. Intercessory prayer through which the Carmelites prayed for the conversion of the world, 'the zeal for souls' as they called it, were one such form, a form which appealed to Teresa particularly in an age when 'heretics' were seen as a dreadful threat to the Catholic Church. Thérèse had been following in the same tradition when she prayed for the murderer Pranzini.

The act of intercessory prayer led to a concern for the outside world, if not always a very realistic understanding of what was going on in it, and a deep wish to relieve some of its suffering and redeem some of its evil. Deprived of other contact with the world the Carmelite nun offered not only her prayers, but her penances and mortifications for the good of others. Hunger and cold, sickness and frustration, the snubs and rebukes and disappointments and humiliations of her life were her 'work' for the world as much as her prayer.

It is not difficult to see some of the features of Carmelite life which had drawn young Thérèse as she had watched and studied it over the years, going to sit in the parlour to talk to her sisters and to Mother Marie de Gonzague, praying in the Carmelite Church, receiving letters from Pauline telling of her deep joy in the life and recommending 'practices' to her little sister. The deep respect with which the Martin family regarded religion, the frustrated ambition of both parents to join religious orders, the visits with her father to the reserved sacrament in the Carmelite church, the drama of her beloved Pauline 'giving up everything' to enter Carmel (accompanied as it was with deep pain for Thérèse) had all combined to make the life desirable.

Thérèse had a feeling for high drama, with herself at the centre of it, earning 'gloire' in one way or another. Of the two careers open to her, as wife and mother or as nun, not a great deal of 'gloire' seemed at first sight to be available, but at least the second offered a kind of hidden 'gloire'. Her yearning for the heroic, for self-sacrifice, for something bigger and more exciting than the humdrum realities of life in a provincial French town, meshed with the wilful self-abandon, the high ideals, the element of 'noblesse' in Carmelite spirituality. By shutting herself away in such a spectacular way, by surrendering the normal small joys and pleasures of life as well as the bigger ones such as freedom, sexuality, and childbearing, she changed from being an ordinary girl into being, in a paradoxical way, somebody. It was as if she had become the heroine of a novel.

The life suited Thérèse, of course, on far more than this romantic level. Already deeply involved in a sense of relationship with God, in particular with Jesus, now she felt that she would at last have time to know God better, to deepen the love she felt, as well as to pray for the conversion of more souls. She had always enjoyed liturgical practices, was never happier than when at Mass or reciting prayers. She had had little interest in men, and none, so far as we know, in the idea of sex or of bearing children. If ever a girl was suited to being a nun, Thérèse seemed to be that girl.

It is not easy to work out from her autobiography quite what the experience of Carmel was like for her once she had settled into the routine. After all her dreaming about it, it would be rather surprising if the reality had not come as something of a disappointment. She, however, insists that this was not so, that she had had no illusions about it, and that the life was exactly what she had expected. Almost in the next breath she speaks of suffering, of how 'those first footsteps of mine brought me up against more thorns than roses', a circumstance which seems much more likely than that an idealistic girl should have her illusions all preserved.

What is striking about the Carmelite timetable to the eyes of any outsider is how lacking in variety it is. Long hours of prayer relieved only by work, sleep, and a minimum of conversation, seem an odd regime for anyone, but particularly for a teenage girl. It is one in which the volatile emotions of adolescence, the need for inner exploration and the discovery of personal identity can have little place except in relation to God, or in limited relationship with other nuns. Similarly the adolescent growth into independence, limited as this was for nineteenth-century girls, is also made impossible by the enclosed environment which Thérèse was never again to leave, as well as by the emphasis on obedience.

Perhaps her desperate need for security, for a home from which important figures could not go away and leave her as successive mothers had done, more than compensated for her losses, at least at the beginning. There was the great pleasure of settling down to what she was quite sure was her life's work – loving God in as direct a way as possible. Then too, the life, despite, or maybe because of, its austerity, had great beauty, with its silence and its contrasts, with the feasts of the Christian year passing in splendid procession, with its intimate knowledge of the seasons, of heat and cold, of darkness and light. It was nobler, if only because so much simpler and, in a sense, more natural, than life in a cluttered and heated drawing-room. The clothes, the ritual, the 'stability' of being always in one place, the simple order of it all, had an undeniable grace.

Thérèse responded to the life as to the one thing she had always been waiting for. She does not complain of boredom, nor of resentment of her chosen imprisonment, though she does, rather pathetically, say how much she misses seeing wild flowers grow in the fields. Once the first exciting newness of it all has worn off, however, she will complain, as so many religious before and since, of *accidie*, a sort of depression in which life is drained of meaning. For her this bears no relation to the constrictions of the life, nor the anger that on some level she may feel about them. She insists that it comes, like all her feelings, directly from God.

What, we wonder, constituted the 'thorns', the suffering at the beginning of her life in Carmel of which she speaks so poignantly? Certainly manual work formed one of her early problems. The Carmelite choir sisters (the more educated women who sang the Office) did not do the hardest forms of work – scrubbing, digging, etc., they had lay sisters, peasant women of little education, who performed those – but they washed clothes, swept floors, laid tables and sewed. Thérèse, so ill-prepared by her sisters to deal with the practical chores of life, suffered a lot over her incompetence at such tasks, and at the impatient and cutting remarks made by other nuns about her awkwardness. She had been brought up to be helpless, and now suddenly, just when she longed so much to be a good nun, she could not manage simple tasks that others performed easily. It was humiliating.

Then again it was difficult for her having a Novice Mistress, Sister Marie of the Angels, who, while being thoroughly kind, was not in the least *simpatico* and who could make almost nothing of Thérèse's form of spirituality. Thérèse throve on intuitive understanding and withered in the cold blast of incomprehension. The Rule obliged her to speak daily of her spiritual concerns to Sister Marie of the Angels, and daily she blushed and stuttered and struggled, unwilling to speak of her experiences, and knowing in advance that the advice she was given was not what she needed.

It seems possible that even Pauline, yearned over from afar during the long years she had been in the convent and no longer available to her little sister, may have been a bit of a disappointment, now that, to a degree, she was permanently accessible. She still tended to see Thérèse as a little girl, as if their relationship was fixed for ever at the point when she had left home, whereas for Thérèse becoming a Carmelite was synonymous with being grown-up, or at least trying to be.

There was certainly one person in the convent who had the intelligence and the spiritual knowledge to respond to Thérèse in the way she wished – the Prioress, Mother Marie de Gonzague. Her position in the convent, to which she had been elected, automatically endowed her with total authority since the nuns had taken vows of obedience. But her influence went far beyond the importance of her office. Of aristocratic background, attractive and educated, Reverend Mother was a strong and autocratic personality who commanded enormous attention. In the restricted emotional life of the enclosure it is clear that some of the nuns were more than a little in love with her. In spite of the general fears about 'special friendships' which were such a feature of the religious orders of the time, and in spite of teachings about 'detachment', it seemed to be natural and allowable to be emotionally fixated on 'Mother'; at any rate Mother herself did little to discourage the process, in fact in subtle ways she encouraged it, picking certain nuns to take care of her during her numerous illnesses, making it clear, in arbitrary fashion, that she preferred some to others. No doubt many of the feelings held by the nuns about their actual mothers, both good and bad, got projected onto Mother Marie.

It would have taken a far more mature personality than Thérèse's not to get drawn into the emotional web that surrounded Reverend Mother. Scarcely out of the period of the schoolgirl crush, possibly still searching for her lost mother, lacking others with whom to share her peculiar kind of spiritual intensity, it was inevitable that she would share in the ardent love that a group of the nuns felt for the Prioress.

If the Prioress had responded straightforwardly to Thérèse's feelings, showing gentle encouragement in her struggles, interest in her spiritual preoccupations, and quietly suggesting the ways in which she was going wrong, Thérèse might have grown in the relationship and been spared much of the suffering of the first years.

As it was, Mother Marie, pleading, of course, that everything she did was for the nuns' spiritual good, made a capricious and sometimes cruel use of power. She showed favouritism to some nuns and took pleasure in making others feel rejected by her. Among those rejected was Thérèse. Reverend Mother was harsh with her, rebuking her frequently, often with sarcasm; Thérèse said ironically that she had only to see Reverend Mother to find herself kissing the floor. Naive, sensitive, idealistic, coming from a home where she had been much petted and admired, Thérèse suffered acutely.

Reverend Mother's excuse was precisely that Thérèse had been spoiled at home. Point was given to this observation by the fact that Pauline and Marie, always accustomed to take care of

Thérèse, and convinced of her 'delicacy' since her childhood illness, could not stop fussing over her, and frequently requested special dispensations for her. In her first winter at Carmel, before she had taken the habit, they arranged for fur boots to be sent in for her ('Thérèse feels the cold so badly'), an annoying intervention for one trying to practise austerity.

Then, too, the precious way Thérèse had been brought up probably made her more than a little hypochondriacal, not least because she suffered a good deal from illness. Thérèse continually reported stomachaches to the Prioress (the Rule did, in fact, require her to report illness to her superiors) until she was crushingly rebuked for being so interested in herself.

Mother Marie had got a little princess on her hands which was not an easy situation to deal with, especially as Pauline, who was obliquely critical of Reverend Mother's way of handling Thérèse, was emerging as the leader of a rival group in Carmel. Mother was beginning to wonder, as well she might, at the wisdom of taking three sisters from one family; the Martin family had a way of sticking together.

But the very real difficulties of being Prioress do not excuse the misery she inflicted on Thérèse who, it was plain for anyone to see, was in love with her. Much later Thérèse wrote painfully of her days as a postulant, of how she would think of excuses (permissions to do this or that) to go into Reverend Mother's office just to see her and talk to her for a moment – 'a crumb of comfort' as she puts it. She fought her longing, sometimes clinging to the banisters to prevent herself from following her inclination.

Another novice, who had followed her into the convent, was soundly rebuked by Thérèse for her affection for Reverend Mother with a degree of righteous indignation that speaks volumes for her own bitter struggles with her feelings.

Her ingenuous habit of pointing out other people's faults to them, even outside the Chapter of Faults, did not make people like Thérèse any better. She came across as a goody-goody, her daddy and sisters' darling, and a religious know-all who seemed to feel she had a hot line to Jesus. It was very irritating. What seems to emerge is that, after the first welcome, Thérèse was not really very popular with her Sisters in religion. As a result of her loneliness and wretchedness as a schoolgirl she had never grown confident in the art of getting along with people outside her family. Knowing that she was an oddity she was sharp and defensive in relations to others. Other girls had never seemed to like her much, for reasons that were not entirely clear to her, and she had resigned herself to a certain sort of loneliness, a habit which stood her in quite good stead in the loneliness of life in a Carmelite convent. But whatever her problems in relationship, and however unfortunate her family's interventions, there was something that impressed the nuns about Thérèse in spite of themselves. Her commitment was greater than most of theirs, something to which they gave their respect, if somewhat grudgingly.

One faithful friend to her was old Mother Geneviève. In her very first half hour in Carmel Thérèse had been aware of Mother Geneviève kneeling in the choir praying for her. Again and again the aged nun showed her that she cared and understood about her struggles, as if she saw her own youthful self in the anguished young novice.

Mother Geneviève's maturity and balance seem to have been unusual. Most descriptions of the life of Carmel and its relationships at this period suggest an emotional hothouse in which tiny incidents were inflated beyond all reason, or in which nerves were frayed to breaking point and beyond.

Reverend Mother was the emotional centre of many people's lives. For Mother to be too unwell to come to Recreation caused her, Thérèse tells us, the most acute disappointment. What she continually longed for was to be able to spend time talking to Reverend Mother and best of all to be able to talk about her spiritual concerns with her – spiritual direction, as it was called. Some nuns had this privilege. Thérèse had to make do with a sharp yes or no when she formally asked for a permission, or a stinging criticism of the way she was cleaning the stairs or weeding the garden. Once she had the job of returning the keys of the grille to Reverend Mother's room. Looking forward to the brief exchange of words when she got there she was disappointed to find another nun there. Thérèse insisted she must hand over the keys to Reverend Mother herself. The other nun said that was impossible since Reverend Mother was ill and asleep. Thérèse wrangled over the matter, using the excuse of obedience to get her own way, until at last Reverend Mother emerged from her sickbed to claim the keys in person. It is impossible to read this without feeling the emotional poverty of Thérèse's life at the time, the desperate longing for warm human contact, and the consequent sadness and loneliness when this was denied and she returned to her silent cell.

It was, of course, in being 'Alone with the Alone', in experiencing the moment of pain or joy as they detached themselves from earthly loves, that the Carmelites were supposed to fulfil their vocation. Remembering, years later, her longing for love in the early days, Thérèse was inclined to say that it was good that she had been treated so harshly, that she had had to endure the 'firm discipline' of Mother, that her 'little flower' had seen no sunshine to speak of, but had been watered by the 'waters of humiliation'. She had learned to live – without praise, encouragement, sympathy or love.

What Thérèse writes suggests that although at the beginning of her time in Carmel, she was obsessed with Mother (as with her history she might well have been), later, from sheer necessity, she worked to a position of emotional independence. Certainly in the pages addressed to Mother Marie towards the end of the autobiography we catch a glimpse of a mature Thérèse who can offer both affection and cool criticism to the adored superior with an even hand. But before that we may guess there was a long period when the lonely and emotionally smitten little girl suffered a great deal from Reverend Mother's treatment of her, and that in this she found the thorns she so poignantly describes. Even after Thérèse had learned detachment Mother Marie still behaved towards her in a punitive and unsympathetic way.

Given Thérèse's total dedication to the religious life, her passionate attempt to be a good nun with every fibre of her being, we may wonder why Mother Marie behaved as she did. No doubt if we could ask her she would say that it was a method of training, and that because Thérèse's vocation was a remarkable one there was all the more reason to be exacting and stern with her, to be sure of bringing her to a state of perfection.

At the same time she must often have been irritated at the intervention of Thérèse's sisters on her behalf, at their pleas for special treatment and dispensations for a child who had freely chosen to enter Carmel and was perfectly fit and well. Maybe she thought Thérèse had put them up to it, maybe she worked her exasperation at them off on Thérèse. It later emerged that she was very jealous of Pauline's status in the community, and it also seems likely that in a community of around twenty-five, three sisters from one family, later to be followed by another sister and a cousin, may have seemed a threat to the balance of power.

Her fears and moods are understandable enough, but it is impossible to forget that, once elected, a Reverend Mother had absolute power. Nuns are not exempt from the danger of absolute power corrupting absolutely and reading of the almost flirtatious way Mother Marie alternately approached and neglected Thérèse, and her extraordinary talent for doing or saying the hurtful thing, it is impossible for a modern reader not to observe a sado-masochistic pattern at work. It is to Thérèse's credit that instead of being drawn further and further into this hateful game, she grew to a place in which Mother's torments could no longer touch her. But not quickly, or easily. Easily depressed, she was sometimes wretched to the point of melancholia. On one such occasion she went to visit old Mother Geneviève as she lay on her sickbed, Thérèse in such deep spiritual darkness that she even doubted the love of God. The old woman drew her to her, gazed deeply at her and said 'Serve God with peace and with joy; remember, always, that our God is a God of peace.' Thérèse went away deeply comforted.

She often needed this sort of personal attention, rarely as it was forthcoming. In the unheated rooms she suffered terribly from the cold, and in winter was often unable to sleep because of it. Her nerves, unstrung by tiredness and silence, were often irritated past endurance by the small noises – the shufflings, fidgetings and throat-clearings – made repeatedly by Sisters in choir. At the big communal washtub where nuns stood round in a circle scrubbing the sheets, she suffered, as they all did, from the hot noonday sun beating down on her thickly-clad body, and she had the conviction that other nuns splashed her with dirty water on purpose. She suffered too under the castigations of a crippled old nun, Mother Peter, whom she had to help make the painful journey from choir to refectory, leaning heavily on Thérèse who always went too slow or too fast. Once in the refectory she settled her with difficulty at the table, and cut up her food for her. The old nun, often in pain, was sharp with her, though she gradually became fond of her and dependent on her.

There were many good moments, moments of luminous prayer, of transparent joy, of almost lightheaded happiness. In May, a month after she had joined the community, her sister Marie made her profession, taking the name of Sister Marie of the Sacred Heart. Thérèse herself crowned her with the traditional bridal wreath. The following January, the Chapter 'received' Thérèse, permitting her to become 'clothed', that is to wear the dress of a Carmelite novice. A photograph was taken of her on this day of days wearing the long brown habit of wool with the rosary at the waist, and the white veil of those who have not yet taken life vows. She looks plump and rather jolly, still very much the schoolgirl hiding an irrepressible grin.

The clothing ceremony had very nearly had to be postponed. Soon after Marie's profession, and only a few months after Thérèse had left him, Louis had had some kind of seizure, perhaps a second stroke, or possibly a fit that presaged a mental breakdown. Whichever it was he had been seriously confused, at times mad, a fact which brought the Martin sisters grief and, it would seem, embarrassment. He had borne the loss of the beloved Thérèse with extreme nobility, writing to friends that 'that little queen of mine, Thérèse, entered Carmel yesterday. It's the sort of sacrifice only God could ask of one. No, don't offer me any sympathy; my heart is overflowing with happiness.' The collapse in his health does not seem the likely outcome of extreme joy but rather of emotions repressed and denied. A cruel twist was that while the daughter he loved so passionately had disappeared forever into Carmel, Léonie, such a trial to her parents, had returned from her unsuccessful stay with the Visitation nuns. The daughter he wanted was gone, and the daughter he didn't want had returned.

With the extraordinary capacity to pull themselves together in times of need – a feature of the Martin family – Louis managed to gather his wandering wits in time for his daughter's clothing and to appear on the day looking composed and handsome, although he was reeling under yet another blow. Céline, who had been his nurse during his recent illness, had now informed him that, like her sisters, she intended to join the Carmelite order.

Thérèse was tremendously excited to have reached 'clothing'. To her delight there was an unexpected shower of snowflakes as white as her veil. Born in January she liked to think of herself as a white winter flower.

At the end of the ceremonies she kissed her father and went back to the snow-covered cloister garth and the little statue of the Child Jesus amid its flowers and lights. She decided that the snow was a betrothal present from Jesus. The Bishop of Bayeux, who had come for the ceremony, stayed to talk with her in obvious admiration for her sense of vocation.

A month later Louis Martin had a more serious attack, and seemed not to know who he was. Thérèse reports it as 'such a wretched, such a humiliating experience' for him. He was confined for a time in an asylum at Caen where Céline and Léonie went to look after him. His health improved after a while – there is a photograph of him in an invalid carriage surrounded by relatives and his two remaining daughters – but from then until his death in 1894 he was to move, with temporary remissions, into deeper states of darkness and helplessness. The chief burden of caring for him was borne by Céline and Léonie, but the three sisters in the convent seemed to feel, oddly, that they were the ones marked out for suffering. Mental illness, whatever the cause, carried a stigma which was uncomfortable.

Thérèse says that 'words couldn't do justice to our feelings', though, of course, 'those three years of Papa's cruel torment were years of great value, of great spiritual profit to his family.'[45] Mother Geneviève, loving as ever, seemed to be the only Sister who fully understood and sympathised.

Meanwhile convent life continued as usual. After taking the habit Thérèse had begun work in the refectory, where Pauline was also working. She tidied, cleaned, laid and cleared tables, distributed water, bread and beer. She claimed that the refectory was a good place for trampling self-love under foot. She tried hard to do that in other ways too.

She struggled with her disappointment when a favourite water jug she had been allowed to keep in her cell was allocated to someone else and she got an old chipped one in its place. She was rebuked for the breaking of a jug which she had not broken at all, and kissed the ground without making an excuse. She tried to inflict various kinds of penances or mortifications on herself, like not leaning back in her chair, but if these were noticed she got rebuked for them.

On one level all the examples she gives of her struggles seem rather foolish, the minutiae of a life so narrow that trifles assumed a vast importance. There was something disconcertingly out of perspective about much that happened at the Lisieux Carmel – it is tempting to wonder how these Sisters would have coped with a job or a family – yet there is a sense in which Thérèse is right. It is the details of life which hurt or which give us joy, which are the straws which tell us what is really going on in our hearts and our souls. With a childlike candour and her usual thin-skinned sensitivity Thérèse notes painfully that 'you got no thanks for doing your duty, unless you were prepared to stick up for yourself, whereas the mistakes you made became public property at once!'[46] She was not without a childish lust for the sort of revenge in which the grown-ups would feel sorry. 'All these things', she pondered, 'would come out on the Day of Judgement.'

Thérèse, like her Sisters in religion, saw this period between 'taking the habit' and her profession, as a betrothal period. Few of them can perhaps have pursued this idea as literally as she did. When she was told that her profession – the 'wedding' – which was due to take place a year after her taking the habit, would be postponed (maybe because of her youth, or maybe because of Louis's illness) she was very upset but told Jesus that she would not ask him to change this arrangement. 'I'm ready to wait just as long as you want me to; only it mustn't be through any fault of mine that this union between us has to be put off . . . I know quite well that nothing in heaven or earth will prevent you from coming to me, and making me, once and forever, your bride.' In what she believes to be the correct attitude of a bride-to-be she says, of Jesus, 'After all, I'd given myself over to our Lord for his pleasure, his satisfaction, not mine.'[47]

She consoled herself, in the long wait for profession, in preparing what she called her 'wedding dress'. Nuns making their profession did approach the altar in a white dress with a gauzy wedding-veil and a bridal wreath made of roses. Thérèse's dress would be made of white silk trimmed with swansdown, and her long fair hair would be curled for the occasion. It is not this dress she had in mind when preparing for her 'wedding' however, but one 'all set with jewels'. By jewels, she says, she means 'trials' – Papa's illness, the disappointment that he could not come to see her make her profession, the emotional dryness of the retreat she made before the great day.

A striking thing happened on the eve of her profession. Making the Stations of the Cross she suddenly, and for the first time, had a clear vision (which she ascribed to the Devil) that her vocation was 'a mere illusion. I still saw life at Carmel as a desirable thing, but the devil gave me the clear impression that it wasn't for me . . . Darkness everywhere; I could see nothing and think of nothing beyond this one fact, that I'd no vocation. I was in an agony of mind.'

She did what a nun should do and reported the feeling to her Novice Mistress. Even as she began to describe it it vanished. Still worried perhaps, Thérèse rehearsed it all again for Reverend Mother who 'only laughed'. Only Mother Geneviève was to tell the girl later, that she too had had similar torturing doubts before taking her final vows.

The next morning, 8 September, Thérèse walked up the aisle to take her vows. As was the custom she had written out her 'billet de profession', and wore it under her dress against her heart. A sort of declaration of purpose, it read:

Jesus, my heavenly Bridegroom, never may I lose this second robe of baptismal innocence; take me to yourself before I commit any wilful fault, however slight. May I look for nothing and find nothing but you and you only; may creatures mean nothing to me, nor I to them – you, Jesus, are to be everything to me. May earthly things have no power to disturb the peace of my soul; that peace is all I ask of you, except love; love that is as infinite as you are, love that has no eyes for myself, but for Jesus, only for you. Jesus, I would like to die a martyr for your sake, a martyr in soul or in body; better still, in both. Give me the grace to keep my vows in their entirety; make me understand what is expected of one who is your bride. Let me never be a burden to the community, never claim anybody's attention; I want them all to think of me as no better than a grain of sand, trampled under foot and forgotten, Jesus, for your sake. May your will be perfectly accomplished in me, till I reach the place you have gone to prepare for me. Jesus, may I be the means of saving many souls; today, in particular, may no soul be lost, may all those detained in Purgatory win release. Pardon me, Jesus, if I'm saying more than I've any right to; I'm thinking only of your pleasure, of your contentment.[48]

The ceremony passed happily. Thérèse seemed to be carried along on a tide of interior peace. The long curls were cut and she made her vows. When the ceremony was over she laid the bridal wreath at the foot of Our Lady's statue. She made the present of a flower in bud to the statue of the Child Jesus. When it grew dark she gazed up at the stars promising herself that soon she would join her heavenly Bridegroom in joy everlasting.

The day appointed for the final ceremony of 'taking the veil', of exchanging the white headdress of the novice for the black one of the professed nun, and of assuming her full name in religion – Thérèse de l'Enfant Jésus et de la Sainte Face – was

24 September. (Like her sister, Pauline, she had started to spend much time gazing and meditating upon the face of the dying Jesus.) On this occasion she felt very tearful and orphaned. Papa could not come, the Bishop who had become a kind of surrogate father and who had promised to come was ill, and Père Pichon was in Canada. A few days after Thérèse took the veil, her cousin Jeanne Guérin got married. With a rather sickening coyness Thérèse tells us that, on Jeanne's visit to the convent, she studied her well to learn 'all the little attentions which a bride ought to lavish on her bridegroom'. She also used Jeanne's wedding invitation as a model for a mock invitation of her own.

Almighty God, Creator of heaven and earth, Lord of the whole world, and the glorious Virgin Mary, queen of the heavenly court, invite you to take part in the wedding of their son Jesus Christ, King of Kings and Lord of Lords, to Thérèse Martin, now invested by right of dowry with two freedoms, those of the Sacred Infancy and of the Passion.[49]

It is not a modest exercise.

Very soon after Thérèse's profession Mother Geneviève died. It was the first death-bed Thérèse had attended and she watched with interest, noting with surprise her own inability to have any feelings about it at all until the very moment when Mother Geneviève died, when she was filled with joy. Believing Mother Geneviève a saint the Sisters were eager to preserve relics of her. Thérèse removed a teardrop from the dead woman's cheek on to a piece of fine linen and forever afterwards carried it round her neck in the locket in which she kept her vows. Soon afterwards she dreamed that Mother Geneviève was making her will, that she had given everything she had away to the Sisters and there was nothing left for Thérèse. But suddenly the old woman had raised herself in bed and repeated three times, in a penetrating voice 'To you, I leave my heart.'

Chapter Seven

THE LITTLE WAY

Thérèse was now approaching her nineteenth birthday. At the beginning of 1892 she was put in charge of the sacristy, the job she liked best of all the jobs in the convent, since she loved to touch the sacred vessels and prepare the altar linen 'for our Lord's coming'. But suddenly the convent was hit with the scourge of influenza and several nuns died – no doubt the poor diet and the bitter cold of the unheated rooms scarcely helped recovery. Thérèse, with a couple of other nuns, alone escaped the plague. With a new strength and aplomb she found herself nursing the sick, organising funerals, and laying out the dead. Thérèse's birthday was marked by the death of one nun, and two more followed in quick succession. One day Thérèse had a presentiment that Sister Madeleine had died, and going into her room found her lying dead on her pallet fully dressed. Sisters already in a state of desperate weakness dragged themselves up to help others worse off. There was one funeral after another.

It is difficult not to feel that Thérèse enjoyed the drama of all this in what was otherwise a very uneventful life. She enjoyed the sense of being useful and practical, someone to whom others turned for help for a change. On a different level she was pleased that because of the danger to life she could receive Communion every day – something unusual in those days.

She noticed at about this time that her old scruples were much less troublesome. She cheerfully admits to her thoughts often wandering during her prayers and to occasional periods of nodding off. The religious life had loosened her up in this important respect.

She had also been lucky in finding a priest who understood her and to whom she felt she could really open her heart. She had been going through one of her bad times, even to the point of doubting whether heaven actually existed, but knew from of old that no one would listen to her fears. Going into the confessional at a retreat (a period of withdrawal from the common life for private recollection), however, she found to her surprise that she could open her heart and felt herself understood 'with an insight that was surprising, almost uncanny'. Pouring out her fears and scruples, her terror of somehow dropping out of the sight of God and being lost (as she had been lost when Zélie died, and when Pauline had left her?) she received a response that totally reassured her. Speaking as a representative of God, the priest said, using every ounce of his authority to comfort her, 'I assure you that He is well satisfied with what you are doing for Him.' The loneliness of convent life with the carping criticism of Reverend Mother and the abrasiveness of daily contact with her fellow-nuns suddenly fell away. Thérèse felt appreciated, loved, caressed, in the way that she needed so badly.

Nowadays she was allowed to do more congenial work in the convent. She redecorated the chapel, she acted as an assistant store-keeper, she became 'Tourière' – the sister who operated the revolving hatch through which presents and communications of all kinds entered Carmel from the outside world, a job which gave her a little external contact. In her spare time she began writing poetry and doing some painting. The poetry lacked originality of expression and when it was not a purely pious theme tended to be a nostalgic recollection of life in the old days at Les Buissonets. Her painting, like every other form of self-expression, was pressed into religious service. She painted a coat of arms to be shared between herself and Jesus, a *jeu d'esprit* of heavy solemnity and humourlessness. The life of Carmel did not seem to encourage great art.

In 1893, to Thérèse's great delight, her sister Pauline, Sister Agnes, was elected Reverend Mother in Mother Marie de Gonzague's place. It was, says Thérèse, a golden day 'that

Pauline should stand, in my life, for our Lord's earthly representative'. The election in fact had nearly split the convent in two with factions rooting for each of the two powerful leaders, and Mother Marie de Gonzague openly sulking when she failed to be re-elected. Thérèse was appointed assistant to the Novice Mistress.

In 1894, Céline, released by the sudden death of Louis in July, entered Carmel as Thérèse had all along been determined that she should. Any attempt by Céline to choose another life for herself was circumvented by Thérèse's formidable determination. When Céline tried to go to a dance Thérèse 'wept in torrents' and prayed vigorously against the undertaking, so much so, Thérèse reports with smug satisfaction, that the young man who accompanied her 'simply couldn't get her to take the floor. There was nothing for it but to take her back to her place.' Thérèse is serenely unworried by any thought of moral blackmail over this episode, as she quite cheerfully admits to having foiled a plan of Père Pichon that Céline should join his mission in Canada. (She is also shameless about having 'prayed down' a sister who, not without reason, thought that three Martin sisters in one community were quite enough.) Thérèse had, as she says, 'this cherished dream . . . that Céline should enter Carmel, our Carmel. It seemed like a dream too good to be true, that I should ever be able to live under the same roof again with my childhood's playmate . . .' What she would do, Thérèse decided, was to offer 'dear Céline, fresh and graceful as a nosegay of flowers, to the same Master's service'.[50] Nothing, not Céline's own wishes, those of a cherished priest or a fellow-sister, counted beside such a dream. Thérèse had a will of iron. By September Céline was safely in Carmel.

As always the contradictions of Thérèse's nature strike us, the extraordinary egotism buried in the claims of self-abandonment. Like a wife who might hesitate to demand something for herself but will do it unhesitatingly if she feels it is for her husband, Thérèse has no qualms about manipulating other people if she can persuade herself that it is what her husband Jesus would like. The self-deception of this – the hidden will to power – is distasteful.

To read Thérèse's writing is to feel that Carmel gave an inadequate outlet for her energies and her intelligence. It lacked stimulus, challenge, the opportunity for physical exercise and virtually all opportunity for what might be called 'play'. Life was solemn, dull, uneventful, silent, a kind of middle age imposed on an ardent girl. Naturally enough Thérèse, always an imaginative child, turned to fantasy as consolation.

In addition to fantasies of herself as the 'little wife' of Jesus or as his childhood plaything, she had always been given to fantasies of herself as crusader or martyr. Now these day-dreams returned, together with poignant pictures of herself as priest, apostle, missionary traveller, Pontifical Zouave dying on the battlefield in defence of the Church. In these intense dreams she represses entirely her knowledge of what it is that debars her from a rich active life – being born a woman with its disappointing weight of social disability – and fancies herself truly eligible, as a man would be, for the adventure she craves.

She feels as if 'she could never satisfy the needs of my nature without performing . . . every kind of heroic action at once'. If she were a priest

how lovingly I'd carry you in my hands when you came down from heaven at my call; how lovingly I'd bestow you upon men's souls . . . I long to enlighten men's minds as the prophets and doctors did; I feel the call of an Apostle. I'd live to travel all over the world, making your name known and planting your cross on heathen soil.'[51]

But more than all these ambitions she longed to die for Jesus, to shed her blood to the last drop.

Martyrdom was the dream of my youth, and this dream has grown in the sheltered world of Carmel . . . A single form of martyrdom would never be enough for me, I should want to experience them all. I should want to be scourged and crucified as you were; to be flayed alive like St Bartholomew, to be dipped in boiling oil like St John . . . offering my neck to the executioner like St Agnes and St Cecily, and, like my favourite Joan of Arc, whispering your name as I was tied to the stake.[52]

The drama of martyrdom, the masochism and orgasmic

excitement of total abandonment, the siren call of death, all beckon the young woman away from the sombre reality of life towards the lurid colours of imagination. Eventually the frustration of disappointed imagination pushed her back again towards another struggle with reality, and it is one which rewards her greatly.

Reading St Paul she dwells on the famous saying that the purpose of life is love (not heroics), and it is as if Jesus himself has spoken to her telling her that her vocation is love and that it can be realised right here and right now. In a transformation of her masochism she evolves her 'Little Way' or 'Little Doctrine' as her sister Marie liked to call it, a path as straightforward and liveable as her fantasies of being boiled in oil were perverse and fantastic.

The Little Way meant trying to get on with life as it actually was, living it with kindness, unselfishness, detailed care – 'always doing the tiniest thing right, and doing it for love'. It was, in some curious way, the reversal of everything she had been taught, the inflated form of Christianity with its dreams of sanctity and martyrdom. Now she saw that all you were asked to do was to follow the will of God, whatever it might be, and to give yourself unreservedly to *that* life and to no other. In a moment of revelation she realised that instead of trying to be something she was not – a crusader or an Apostle – she was now free to be Thérèse with all her little problems, including the babyishness which she had begun to recognise in herself as a kind of permanent imprint. It was as if she had scraped away years of nonsense and found a fundamental truth which had eluded her by its very simplicity. 'It's love I ask for, love is all the skill I have.' It struck her that her very poverty of gifts and of opportunities might make her a kind of representative of all who were poor and inadequate in the world, but who strove to love God. 'I implore you', she says to Jesus, 'to look down in mercy on a whole multitude of souls that share my littleness.' Praying for those souls, working out the 'Little Way' in her own life were, she saw now, her true vocation, and it was one that filled her with joy. She no longer dreamed of dreadful martyrdoms because she saw that, in the present, without manipulations on her part, her life was already a 'burnt offering' for a purpose she could only dimly understand but knew that she had chosen.

Thérèse's spiritual coming of age had important consequences for the convent since, on becoming Prioress Pauline had appointed Mother Marie de Gonzague as Mistress of Novices, with Thérèse as her assistant. For the first time Thérèse had a job that made use of her abilities and which forced upon her the human contact she had dodged most of her life. There were not many novices, one or two at a time, one of whom was Céline, but Thérèse had to help instruct them, listen patiently to their spiritual and personal difficulties, point out to them the self-deceptions and motions of false pride which motivated them, and generally act with a maturity that had never been required of her before.

It would have been easier to perform the task without being the underling of the sarcastic and fault-finding Mother Marie de Gonzague – the novices, Thérèse felt, took advantage of this situation to play her up a bit, but she was pleased and touchingly proud at finding she could do the job. She realised that her long apprenticeship in the art of unpopularity stood her in good stead; she could point out faults and endure the pique of the novices without worrying too much about being disliked. Perhaps this very fact made them begin to trust her and she found to her delight that they seemed glad to confide in her (maybe because they found Mother Marie too formidable). She was warmed by this human contact and astonished to find herself, for the first time in her life, perceptive about others, sometimes astonishing the novices by strokes of insight about their states of mind. She began to develop a kind of psychological interest in them, as well as a human and spiritual one. 'One thing I've noticed is this,' she says. 'All souls, more or less, have to put up the same sort of fight, but on the other hand no two souls are alike.'[53]

She discovered that different techniques worked with different Sisters. For some of them it was important to know that she too had her fair share of human weakness, so that they could become bold enough to admit their own humiliating defects. Others needed to believe her perfect for a while, and she saw that there was a sort of upside-down humility in bearing with their projections while they found themselves in the religious life. Some needed enormous gentleness, and others strictness and firmness. All of them needed to find her a good example, in that she led the religious life joyfully and with integrity.

She needed to be available for conversation, to know when to be unyielding with a novice who was looking for a loophole to let herself off the recognition of her own pride, to know when to scold and when to let something go.

So much wisdom and good sense in a very young woman shows how much Thérèse had grown up at Carmel, what a long way she had come from Les Buissonets. She was growing to be an important figure in the little community.

In 1894 she wrote a play in verse about her favourite Joan of Arc, not then a saint (she was canonised in 1920, only five years before Thérèse herself) but a much loved French figure with the improbable title of Venerable. On two or three days in the year Carmel discipline was slightly relaxed and on one such day Thérèse's patriotic and pious piece was enacted, with herself playing the part of the saint. Rather surprisingly she was permitted to wear home-made armour over a skirt for the occasion and wear her hair, now grown quite long again, in flowing locks round her shoulders. Céline, wearing her habit, played St Margaret.

During Pauline's term of office as Prioress she suggested that Thérèse start a correspondence with a young seminarian who had written to the convent asking for a Sister to pray for him as he approached ordination and prepared to go out to the mission field. Thérèse had always thought she would like to have a brother who was a priest and she accepted eagerly the task of praying for the young man and writing letters to him. Such requests were not unusual and when Mother Marie de Gonzague received a similar request and invited Thérèse to respond to it, she felt that she now had two brothers, a sort of substitute for the two brothers who had died in infancy.

In December of 1894 Thérèse was launched in an undertaking that was to have tremendous consequences. Sitting chatting with Pauline and Marie one evening, Thérèse was going over some of her favourite memories of childhood. Marie casually suggested that she should write them down. Pauline, momentarily taken with the idea, but knowing that Thérèse would probably never find the time for it, suddenly assumed her official mantle as Prioress, and said 'I order you to write down the memories of your childhood.' Thérèse, obviously surprised, had no choice but to obey.

Her life made little provision for uninterrupted bouts of concentration, but at night when she could have been sleeping she began to write in a school exercise book keeping the pages in a wooden writing desk.

It is not easy to imagine quite why Pauline had issued the order – perhaps merely on a whim – but she had unwittingly given an extraordinary source of pleasure to her sister. With unconcealed enjoyment, and no little literary talent, Thérèse, always so locked in her childhood experience, describes in vivid detail the life of her pious bourgeois French family, first at Alençon, then at Lisieux. She evokes days in the kitchen with her mother and Victoire, games played with Céline, outings with Papa, moments when her big sisters returned from school, the appalling pain of the loss of her mother and of Pauline, the joys and excitements of religion, the pain of school and the pleasures of the family. There is sentimentality and false piety (some of it inserted after her death), moments of sheer silliness and a pervading lack of humour, but nevertheless it is a literary *tour de force*, a piece of writing which carries the reader along fascinated except where it slides into religiosity. Thérèse is, as always, deeply fascinated by herself and her own story, and, unexpectedly, this makes her a wonderful *raconteuse*. We remember that her only success among her playmates at school was her ability to tell a story.

It is difficult to imagine what she felt as she worked at this recapitulation of the family life of the Martins. Her pleasure in writing it suggests that it was a wholesome holiday from 'being religious' – a chance to be simply and naturally herself and to remember happy times. The book took her about a year to write, presumably because she had very little time or energy to work on it, though the style is one of rapt literary concentration. In January 1896, Thérèse carried the completed manuscript into chapel with her, bowed before the stall of the Prioress, her sister Pauline, and laid the sheets down before her, her task completed 'under obedience'.

As it happened Pauline's three-year term as Prioress was completed a week or two later, and by a curious swinging of the pendulum of convent politics which was to make both women alternate leaders of the community for a number of years to come, Mother Marie was restored to the office of Prioress and Pauline had to stand down. In the work of handing over office she did not get a chance to read her sister's manuscript until a couple of months later – one sees her storing it up as a sort of treat at a time of greater leisure. She recognised its quality at once, and thought about the possibility of circulating it among friends of the convent as an exercise of evangelism, but found herself in a dilemma. In this part of her memoirs (Thérèse started a new manuscript soon after, this time addressed to her sister Marie) she had concentrated almost entirely upon the domestic life of the Martins and said very little about the life of the convent. Maybe if Pauline had still been Prioress, as she had probably expected to be, she would have added a few religious conceits to the book and sent it out to friends. But she could not imagine that Mother Marie, wary of the Martin sisters in general and of Mother Agnes in particular, would look kindly upon any scheme that gave them greater publicity. So the manuscript began to gather dust.

Whether Thérèse felt disappointed about this we do not know – like any author she enjoyed her own work and felt secretly that others would like it too. But she had other things on her mind that spring. She kept the full fast of Lent in all its rigour, suffering acutely as always from the cold, but feeling unusually well. On the night of Maundy Thursday, however, she retired to her cell at midnight, after long hours watching in front of the altar of repose, lay down in bed, and at once felt her mouth fill with a warm, sticky substance which she guessed to be blood. She had a longing to light her lamp to verify the fact, but feeling this would be an indulgence, she disciplined herself to wait until morning. The morning light confirmed her guess; her handkerchief was covered in blood. Haemorrhaging from the lungs, she knew very well, was a symptom of disease that was probably mortal. For a long time Thérèse had been half, or more than half, 'in love with easeful death'. Her response was in keeping. The bleeding from her lungs was, she says, a present from Jesus, 'nothing less than the hope of seeing him, quite soon, in heaven'.

When she woke on the fateful Good Friday it was with a sense that good news was coming to her, and in the morning light she 'realised that there was no mistake'. The Bridegroom was on his way.

She was, she says, longing to tell Mother Marie de Gonzague of the event and could scarcely wait until Prime and Chapter of Faults were over. She told Reverend Mother the news, adding that she was in no pain and wanted no special treatment, only to keep the Good Friday fasts and austerities like everybody else. Incredibly Mother Marie saw no reason to argue with this. Already weakened by bleeding, Thérèse went without food and spent the working part of the day washing windows. A novice seeing her at this task and noticing at once that she was ill, without, of course, knowing what had happened, begged her to rest. She did not do so. That night she haemorrhaged once more.

Convent life continued as normal with no mitigation of the Rule for Thérèse. If she had thought that Mother Marie might begin to show the face of love to her in her physical distress she was mistaken. In this the old sado-masochistic pattern between them continued unchanged. Thérèse fell into a severe depression. Heaven no longer seemed a delightfully close possibility but a source of 'conflict and torment', because she could not possibly be worthy of it. The physical exhaustion that accompanies bleeding, the loneliness of facing death without the loving sympathy of others, the hurt of 'Mother's' cruelty, all filled her with despair. Thérèse was only twenty-two and her youth fought hard against the fate prepared for it. She comforted herself as best she could by identifying with all those millions with no torch of faith to guide them in similar suffering. Like Columbus divining the unseen New World and finding his way to it so she, with only intuition left to her, would find her way to heaven and Jesus. Yet the fear that her doubts were blasphemous troubled her dreadfully. She took comfort in the simplicity of the 'Little Way'.

Within a few weeks of the Good Friday discovery Thérèse had a dream of great significance that lifted her out of the 'dark tunnel' of despair. She was not given to dreaming as a rule, except about flowers or fields, and was therefore astonished to see three Carmelite sisters in the dream, one of them the Venerable Mother Anne of Jesus who brought the reformed Carmelite order to France. Her face conveyed an extraordinary beauty and sense of eternity as well as a deep love. Thérèse felt emboldened to ask an important question – Would God come and fetch her soon? Yes, said Mother Anne, very soon. Then, bringing out the other deep, childlike question that always occupied her heart (it was the night-time question of her childhood – 'Was I a good girl?'), Thérèse painfully asked whether God was really satisfied with her 'unimportant little sacrifices', or did he wish something else from her. With a look of deep love, Mother Anne told her that God asked no more. 'He is content with you, well content.' The old sense of the closeness of heaven returned with its comforting reassurance.

But the suffering was very great. Photographs of Thérèse in this phase of her life are disturbing. Unlike the picture of the plump-faced young novice with the eyes of a merry schoolgirl which was taken on the day of her clothing, the later photographs show her with dark shadows under her eyes and a look of inexpressible sadness. Although only six years have passed since the first picture, she looks like a woman twenty years older.

It is not clear exactly when Thérèse contracted tuberculosis. Despite her sisters' fears she had been a strong girl when she entered the convent, and had been one of only two Sisters left on her feet during the great influenza epidemic. Yet just over four years later she was gravely ill. In June 1894, she had suffered from a persistent soreness of the throat which had been treated by cauterisation with silver nitrate. Convent gossip attributed this malaise to too much talking to the novices rather than to anything remotely dangerous.

Institutions such as schools, convents and seminaries were notorious for the high number of deaths from pulmonary tuberculosis; in some institutions, such as the school where two of the Brontë children died, infected milk and water supplies and poor food seem to have both carried infection and weakened resistance. Such deaths were a tragic commonplace.

Knowledge of the essential hygiene to prevent the spread of the disease was not advanced. Patients used the same cups, plates, napkins and towels as healthy people, and no one suspected the dangers of sputum brought up in coughing attacks. On the other hand in France in the late nineteenth century something was known of the importance of rest (it seemed a natural response to the terrible exhaustion of tuberculous patients), of fresh air and of nourishing food. Yet despite the seriousness of her symptoms no particular care was taken of Thérèse. She continued with the rigorous fasting (in itself, perhaps, one of the culprits which had undermined her resistance), with hard physical work and interrupted sleep. In the curious game that she and Mother Marie played with one another there was a kind of grim satisfaction on both sides in not giving way and recognising a special need. Reverend Mother would make special concessions to Thérèse if she would come to her and beg for them. Thérèse, who had learned not to beg for anything from Mother Marie and who had a stubborn determination to live as if she was not ill, would not ask for them. Even though the bone over which they fought was Thérèse's life, two determined people were not going to give way.

The dreadful details of Thérèse's decline were meticulously

charted by a French priest, Etienne Robo, in 1955. His sister had died of tuberculosis in an Ursuline convent in 1904 where she was similarly deprived of necessary care, and in crusading zeal he wrote about the scandal of Thérèse's final illness (a labour which, not surprisingly, angered the Carmelites considerably).

Reminding us that it was the duty of a Prioress to care for her nuns physically as well as spiritually, he asks the question, 'How is it that for twelve months, from March 1896 to April 1897 [Thérèse] received no care, no treatment worth mentioning and was allowed to keep all the Rules without any relaxation?'[54] One of the Sisters during the process of Thérèse's canonisation made the situation perfectly clear. 'In spite of her illness she never exempted herself from devotions in common, nor failed to attend any of the public devotions, nor did she seek exemption from heavy tasks.' She went on without complaining to the end of her strength. 'I can still go about,' she would say, 'I must stay at my post.' It was, of course, seen as an example of heroism, with the question of why she must stay at her post instead of going to bed until she felt better, never asked.

When her cough became worse the local doctor prescribed a bottle of tonic. Whether he also prescribed leaving the window open at night we do not know. Fr. Robo says that in his sister's case this practice was disallowed on the grounds that 'it was not proper for nuns to keep their windows open at night'.

By September 1896 she was sleeping scarcely at all, kept awake by violent fits of coughing that forced her to sit upright in bed. She felt herself fortunate in that her cell stood by itself, next to the Chapter House so that she did not disturb her Sisters. Yet after these sleepless nights she got up unfailingly at five or six in the morning to go to Mass, and would follow this with a day of strenuous chores, doing the washing, maybe, cleaning, decorating, gardening.

We may wonder why Thérèse's natural sisters, always so anxious about her, did not grasp the gravity of her state sooner. The answer is that she concealed it from them (as she was not permitted by the Rule to conceal it from the Prioress). 'My poor little Mother,' Thérèse was to write about Pauline later, 'you must thank God I did not tell you, for, had you been aware of the state I was in and seen me so little cared for, it would have broken your heart.'[55] This inadvertently suggests that Thérèse felt a sense of blame towards the Prioress who did not choose to lift her heavy burden and send her to bed.

Late in 1896 Thérèse was given a mustard plaster late at night (as described by George Orwell in *Down and Out in Paris and London*, an excruciatingly painful form of treatment). She got up and went to Mass as usual. Concerned about her sister's appearance Pauline followed her back to her cell and found her sitting on her stool, leaning against the wall, as if unable to support herself. Why had she gone to choir, Pauline asked her passionately, receiving one of Thérèse's stubborn replies, 'This is not too much suffering for the privilege of Holy Communion.' Yet Communion could easily have been brought to her in her cell or in the infirmary.

So she continued through the bitter winter weather, worn out by her cough, her fever, and her haemorrhages. The infirmarian Sister Marie of the Trinity noticed her condition and went to the Prioress to suggest some mitigation of the Rule for Thérèse. The Prioress was short with her. 'I have never heard before of such young people as this who think of nothing but their health. In former times one would never have thought of missing Matins. If Sister Thérèse of the Child Jesus has come to the end of her strength, let her come and tell me so herself.' So the battle between them continued.

Thérèse justified her tragic obstinacy in terms of obedience. 'Our Mother knows very well that I am tired: it is my duty to tell her what I feel, and since in spite of it she gives me permission to keep step with the community, it must be that she is inspired by God, who wants to grant my wish to go on working to the very end.'

Behind such a statement are unspoken volumes about the relationship between Thérèse and Mother Marie de Gonzague. If Mother Marie was punishing Thérèse by ignoring her mortal illness, then she in turn may punish her by dying.

Chapter Eight

A VERY LITTLE SAINT

During the winter of 1896–7 Thérèse struggled on alone with the terrible inroads of her illness, suffering daily from high fever, bearing the bitter cold of the open cloister and the interminable hours in choir without complaint. Like her mother Zélie who had tried to carry on family life as usual in the final stages of cancer, and who had done her best to conceal her suffering from anyone, Thérèse smiled, held herself upright and lived out the Rule as it was written. Yet fever, a bad cough, pallor, extreme fatigue, are not so easily hidden, we would think, at least not from those who are with us night and day.

By April of 1897 she had become so breathless that one night it took her half an hour to climb the stairs to her cell, and another hour to undress with long pauses for recovery between each action. Beaten at last in the unequal struggle she told the Prioress that she could not carry on. As if to show how generous she could be when appealed to in a properly humble manner Mother Marie at once sent for the doctors and began to organise a succession of expensive treatments. She appointed Céline and Pauline to nurse Thérèse, with her sister Marie allowed to be in constant attendance.

Medical science was, we know now, more or less helpless to treat advanced tuberculosis until the arrival of sulphonamides in the 1940s but this did not prevent a number of measures being tried. In addition to the painful plasters of mustard and belladonna, there was cupping (a treatment which involved raising the flesh of the back here and there with a glass cup), painting of the chest with creosote, and an excruciating process of injecting dozens of needles. The purpose of most of them seems to have been a sort of stimulation – by causing the blood to rush to the afflicted place through the use of hot substances it was hoped the body would be provoked into defensive action which would also destroy the tubercle bacillus.

Meanwhile the patient suffered a terrible wasting, so familiar to us from the description of nineteenth-century deaths, a desperate cough which, as the lungs decayed and hardened, literally brought up fragments of the lung. The result of this was a growing difficulty in breathing at all, extreme fatigue and weakness. Dipping a pen in an inkpot, sewing, holding a book, were often too exhausting. There was also severe pain.

The Prioress who had watched, apparently unmoved, through so many months while Thérèse gradually declined, was now all concern, describing Thérèse as 'the angel of the community', fulsomely praising her on every occasion, weeping freely in chapel when Thérèse was prayed for. Her cruelty had swung into its opposite – sentimentality. For Thérèse, however, it was a matter of great joy that she was once again apparently in favour with 'Mother' – she was touchingly pleased. She saw this as a special gift from Jesus. In the person of Mother Marie he now smiled upon her.

Her lapse into weakness and the official change in the treatment of her made a big difference. The Guérin family now knew of Thérèse's condition and they charged Marie, who had just that year been admitted to Carmel as Sister Marie of the Eucharist, to send them daily reports, in itself a sort of check on the treatment received by her.

For Thérèse the chief comfort of the new state of affairs was the constant attendance of her sisters and the freedom to chat to them as freely as she had done in childhood. Her days were spent in bed, or sitting in a little white armchair, or, when the summer drew on, outside in the cloister or the chestnut walk in the invalid carriage which Louis had used in his last years. The last photograph of Thérèse shows her reclining in this carriage in the cloister, her emaciated face tiny in its starched cap.

Thérèse had not the smallest doubt that she was dying – in

the spring of 1897 she told Céline that she would die 'this very year'. She was impatient for it. 'I am like a small child at the railway station, waiting for its parents to place it on the train. But, alas, they do not come, and the train is leaving. Still, there are other trains . . .' She also compared herself to a child who is longing for a piece of cake and keeps holding out its hand for it, only to find the cake withheld. Picturing death with her usual vivid imagination she wanted to get on with the process. It was to be much more protracted and horrific than even she could possibly guess.

At first, however, there was the relief from the intolerable struggle to live as if she was well, the lift of spirits that came from resting, eating better food, simply giving way to the disease that had her in its power. The beauty of the spring, the release from the dreadful cold of a Carmelite winter buoyed her up for a little. With her sisters she reconstructed some of the precious memories of Les Buissonets.

In June, lying out in the chestnut walk in her chair, she embarked on the final section of her autobiography which she addressed to Mother Marie de Gonzague, perhaps the only human being apart from her own relatives whom she had ever deeply loved. This, like the earlier exercises in autobiography, she wrote under obedience. In the change of climate that had occurred since Thérèse had succumbed to the ravages of her disease Pauline had felt it possible to go to Mother Marie de Gonzague, tell her about the earlier autobiographical writings, and to suggest that Thérèse might now occupy her idle hands writing something about her life as a nun. Pauline knew that it was touch and go whether the Superior would agree or refuse. She immediately agreed.

Thérèse was so weak that she was forced to write in pencil, and even then her handwriting, usually neat, like that of a young schoolgirl, was hard to read. There were other difficulties too. The other nuns, passing her on the way to haymaking and other summer duties, continually interrupted her with friendly conversation and gifts of flowers. Thérèse rather churlishly complains about this in the midst of her writing, objecting that the

flowers would be better still waving on their stalks. Inept as
always in the ways of friendship she misses the point of their
kindness, their oblique attempt to tell her that they love her.

The writing that they interrupted, however, was her own
attempt to express love for Mother Marie, and on page after
page it charts their difficult relationship, hinting at the deep
emotions below the surface, and placing the whole in the
context of Thérèse's life in the convent, and her overwhelming
love for Jesus. It is a difficult terrain, especially for one like
Thérèse who had no aptitude for tact. If she left out the pain
Reverend Mother had dealt her over the years she would distort
their whole history. Yet a diatribe of accusation would be un-
Christian. Besides, the warmth of emotion she feels for this
surrogate-mother often wipes out the resentment and the pain,
particularly in a phase, like her present one, when the face of
love is being turned upon her.

Thérèse solves the problem rather neatly by writing down
many of the incidents in her life with Mother Marie, but offering
fulsome gratitude for the pain involved by suggesting how much
they helped her to grow – which, it might be argued, they did.
Whether all of this material is written quite 'straight', whether
the skilled novice mistress is practising her skill to get a lesson
home without too much loss of face, whether she is engaged on a
self-consciously Christian effort to suppress her angry feelings,
or has just 'smoothed over' her pain is hard to know.

What she claims to feel is an enormous 'gratitude' towards
Mother Marie, as well as a sense of her heart being 'knitted' to
hers. She says that she treats her not at all as a Prioress but
'as a mother'. The severity she has endured at her hands she
describes as 'firm, motherly discipline'. 'I thank you from the
bottom of my heart for not having treated me too gently. Jesus
knew well enough that the Little Flower he had planted was in
need of watering; only the waters of humiliation could revive it
– it was too weak a plant to take root without being helped in
this way. And it was through you, Mother, that this blessing was
bestowed.'[56] She remembers what happened on the unforget-
table Good Friday when she woke up soaked in her own blood.

How she confided to Mother Marie what had happened and how, encouraged by Thérèse, she remitted none of the exacting duties of the day. 'Never had it appealed to me so much, the severe way of practising austerities we have in Carmel.'

Despite the months of neglect Thérèse piles on gratitude for the most recent change of heart.

I am touched by all these motherly attentions of yours; my heart really is overflowing with gratitude, and I shall never forget what I owe you, never. The most touching thing of all is the novena which you're making to Our Lady of Victories, all the Masses you're having said for my recovery. What a wealth of spiritual resources! . . . Mother, look at the life I live here! . . . all I've got to do is to carry out the work you've given me to do, such easy work! And then, all this motherly care you shower on me! I never feel the pinch of poverty; I've always got everything I want. But above all, here at Carmel I have your love and the love of all the Sisters, and it means so much to me! I see in you not merely a mother, greatly loving and greatly loved, but beyond all that Jesus himself . . . Of course, you treat me like a special case, like a spoilt child, so that obedience costs me nothing. But something deep in my heart tells me that I should act just as I do, love you as much as I do, if you saw fit to treat me harshly. I should still know that it was the will of Jesus; you would only be doing it for the good of my soul.[57]

This extraordinary recital of gratitude is difficult reading. Even when we are used to Thérèse's strange inversions so that what is bad is good and what is good is bad, and the puzzling distortions they make in the truth, it is still tempting to say bluntly 'That's a lie! She treated you abominably and you know it!' Yet we may wonder how conscious Thérèse was of the untruthfulness involved. What is most interesting and important about these statements of hers is the way they illustrate how total the dependence of Thérèse had been upon Mother Marie. In her longing to feel loved by this Mother whom it was almost impossible to please (like Zélie?), she survives by denying neglect and harshness, the harshness which, by offering a sort of unanswerable riddle, kept Thérèse bound. There *must* be a way to make Mother Marie love her, Thérèse had felt, as helplessly as a child with a capricious mother. There must be an answer to the riddle which would make her lovable. She would try and never stop trying. Dimly she perceives that her Superior's cruelty to her indicates something special in their relationship – that the two of them are caught up together in a mutual exploration of different aspects of suffering – one of them of power and the other of pain. But in the summer of her illness the rules of this dreadful game seem to have changed, temporarily at least, and in the joy of this fact she writes rapturously of life in the convent and of the spiritual ambition which drives her. She writes with the kind of passionate intimacy, the longing to tell everything, with which another woman might write to her lover. In the sombre and lonely place where she confronts her own death she needs to feel loved and understood; maybe Mother Marie, disturbed and hurtful as she may have been, even in some sense the architect of her present misfortunes, may have seemed like the only contemporary with the intelligence and the insight to enter with her into this final struggle. At the very least it was an invitation to her to do so.

Jesus and Mother Marie are as one person now in Thérèse's mind. Once when Thérèse had felt snubbed and ignored by Mother she had felt that Jesus had decided that the waters of humiliation were what the Little Flower needed to make it grow. Now, in the bitter experience of a dreadful illness in which 'my humiliations have reached the brim', Thérèse felt that Jesus had decided that there was no longer any need for the external application of humiliation, and so he, and Mother, smiled on her, having decided that the plant needed sun to make it grow.

The disease did indeed find ever new forms to distress and to humiliate, coupling extreme weakness, the fight for breath, and the racking cough, with fits of uncontrollable vomiting and pain so severe that the patient was beside herself with agony and longed for nothing but release. She became unable to eat anything but liquid food and even that often filled her with acute nausea. One of the nuns was deeply offended when Thérèse refused a cup of broth she had brought her and stormed away saying that not only was she not a saint as rumour had it in the convent that she might be, she was not even a good nun. One of Thérèse's rare flashes of humour showed at this news. 'What a benefaction', she said, 'to hear on one's death-bed that one has not even been a proper nun!'

She who had never had much interest in food, who had seen it mainly as an opportunity for strengthening her self-control, suddenly felt she was starving, as indeed she was, and had continual fantasies of eating all kinds of delicacy, a phenomenon quite well known in the later stages of her disease. She found the experience deeply shaming, and believed that the devil was doing his best to humiliate her.

She moved in and out of periods of spiritual darkness as her body fought its fierce battle. In June she had had a sort of vision of her faith as a lighthouse beckoning into the harbour of heaven, but this was frequently obscured by her terrible sufferings.

'Oh, how I pity myself', she remarked movingly. 'Nevertheless I would not suffer less.'

She told the Prioress that she had never asked God for suffering, and that therefore it was up to Him to give her the strength to endure it.

'It seems to me you are made for suffering,' Mother Marie replied, truthfully enough. 'Your soul is tempered for it.'

'Oh, for spiritual suffering, yes; I can take a great deal of that . . . But as for physical pain, I am like a little child, a very little child. I cannot think at all, I only suffer, minute after minute.'

Thérèse was not unusual in regressing to the state of 'a litle child' in sickness – it had always been a favourite recourse of hers, in any case. More than once the thought of suicide occurred to her and she warned Pauline about the dangers of leaving poisonous medicine within reach of patients in great pain.

Not knowing how long the agony must go on, but only that it would be terminal, made it worse. In July when she was so much worse that she was moved to the infirmary the chaplain tried to jolly her along by decrying all her talk of entering heaven, an infuriating sort of patronism. Her 'crown' was far from finished, he told her. She replied that although she had not finished it, God had finished it for her.

It occurred to her that death was really much like all the other events in her life that she had looked forward to. Like First Communion, or entering Carmel, or being clothed or professed, it seemed like a longed-for place that she had no idea how to reach. And yet, after all, she *had* reached those other peaks. But in the meantime she had the very human feeling that she did not know how dying was done.

Just as Bunyan's Christian had been much haunted by hobgoblins in the Valley of the Shadow of Death, so poor Thérèse was troubled by the whispering in the darkness, by the sense of supernatural threat and the temptation to despair. A candle burned all night in her room and her bed was sprinkled with holy water. It seemed to her that, like Job, she was being tried by extreme suffering, driven towards the blasphemy of denying her faith. She clung to the thought that God was, and would be, present in the suffering however bad it was. In the heart of the suffering, she claimed, she felt a core of peace, or maybe it was that suffering and joy were, on some deeply mysterious level, the same thing, the two faces of love.

'What do you say to God?' she was asked.

'I say nothing – I just love Him.'

The weariness and pain from moment to moment, the continual fighting for breath, was very terrible. Again the strange role of the Prioress emerges. In August when the usual doctor was on holiday, Dr Néele, her cousin Jeanne's husband, temporarily replaced him. Either because of their relationship, or because he perceived the gravity of Thérèse's condition more clearly, he suggested that he should come every day. The Prioress, seemingly annoyed at this, only allowed him to come three times in all. In addition to her other troubles Thérèse had developed bedsores which made any movement in bed agony. Sitting upright to breathe in attacks of coughing felt like sitting on red-hot iron. On 22 August her intestines began to be very badly affected; drinking a glass of water to assuage her raging thirst felt like throwing water into a furnace. She was beside herself with agony. Dr Néele was not sent for until 30 August.

The regular doctor, Dr de Cornières, returning from his holiday in September, was sufficiently appalled by the suffering of Thérèse to recommend hypodermic injections of morphia. This the Prioress rejected out of hand. The doctor insisted on some syrup of morphia. This too the Prioress deplored and tried to reduce to a minimum, but almost surreptitiously Pauline and Céline offered it in the worst moments. It was not very effective. Many devout writers on the life of Thérèse have excused Mother Marie on the grounds that the use of a drug mitigated the heroism of the Carmelite life. 'Soul-making' took precedence over every other consideration, even, it would appear, the virtue of compassion. It was the last, and the most terrible example, of Mother Marie's form of exercising power.

As so often in the life of Thérèse, in her dying there were puzzling failures of relationship. There is the story of the nun who liked to come and stand at the foot of the bed and laugh at her sufferings. Hagiographers have relished this detail as proving the superhuman patience of Thérèse without discussing the improbability of it or at least what degree of mental derangement it might have indicated in the nun.

Then there was the gossip among the nuns about how 'useless' Thérèse now was, how she was not 'doing' anything, how she was being 'spoiled' once again by her sisters. There was even some suggestion that she was not half as ill as she pretended. When she seemed on one occasion to be near to death her pallet, on which she would be laid for burial, was tactlessly placed outside the door where she could see it. The Sisters are shown as endlessly persecuting her with silly questions about dying, cruel demands for her attention, struggles to obtain relics, as well as envious remarks about the luxury of her present life.

No doubt some visitors stayed too long and were thoughtless, that some pointed remarks were made about how the Martin family had got it together again, and that some irritation was felt at the Martin girls' premature insistence that the youngest Martin was a saint. Anything beyond this in a small community in which one of their number was seen to be suffering acutely seems psychologically unlikely, a distortion that has more to do with a wish to show that Thérèse was perfect than with anything that is humanly probable. Unless, of course, we are to believe that Thérèse had been living in a house of monsters.

Reading between the lines of the considerable amount of material written about Thérèse's death we may wonder if one of the heavier burdens she had to bear was not the attentions of her natural sisters. With the curious spiritual ambition that had always been typical of the Martin family they were very determined that Thérèse should be seen as a saint, and many of their remarks and gestures in her dying weeks were designed to convey to her that nothing less than a sanctified death was expected of her.

Fallen back into the care of the determined big sisters who had, in the words they would have used, 'moulded' her as a child, she had little choice but to try to please. In a thousand ways their expectation was conveyed to her, an expectation which, of course, chimed with a cherished hope of her own. So that day after day between the fever and the pain, the struggle for breath and the vomiting, the question was always being silently asked 'Are we watching the last days of a saint?' It was this ambition which the rest of the community picked up from the Martin sisters, partly believed in (see their determination to obtain relics), and partly mocked.

How did it show itself? In the notebook which Pauline whipped out, time after time, to record the most artless utterances of the tormented invalid, and in the endless questioning of her designed to make pearls drop from her lips. Later in the shameless effort to collect relics – hairs, tears, from her still suffering body. The notebooks which all the sisters kept accumulated an enormous amount of evidence about Thérèse which was later used to make points in the canonisation ceremonies; it is perfectly clear that Pauline had just such a use in mind.

We may find it difficult to think of another saint who had a Boswell, whereas Thérèse had two. Pauline admitted in the

canonisation ceremonies that the note-taking had been painful
and inhibiting for Thérèse, although she had submitted to it out
of love for Pauline. Here, as in the battles over the administra-
tion of morphine, love and compassion take second place to
spiritual ambition, and Thérèse is damagingly exploited. She
complained of those death-bed inquisitions that she suffered,
that she felt like the Maid of Orleans before her accusers.

Her sisters wondered aloud in her hearing whether her body
would decay in death or whether it would remain incorrupt as a
sign of sanctity. They planned the sort of death they thought she
ought to have – joyful and fearless. They seemed worried that
death itself would take too long and thus detract from the
interest and attention being shown her by her relatives and
fellow-nuns. They asked if she thought she would be made an
angel when she got to heaven. They asked, rather oddly, what
she would die of. 'Death,' replied Thérèse succinctly. They
asked if she had an intimation of when she was to die. She had
none. They cried out that she was indeed a saint.

The question of sanctity was, as always, the unanswerable
conundrum. If she said she was a saint she would be guilty of the
sin of pride and therefore would not be one. If she said she was
not a saint and actually was one, then, out of false modesty, she
would be guilty of a lie. In practice, since sanctity is accompanied by a lack of all egotism, the saint is unlikely to spend
time wondering if she or he is a saint – only if asked the cruel
question do they have to struggle with the meaningless idea.
Thérèse had longed so much to be a saint in her youth, and
knew how greatly her sisters' hopes were pinned to the idea.
The listlessness of her replies to their questions suggests that
in pain and weariness the matter did not interest her as much
as formerly.

She began by saying that far from being a saint she was only a
very little soul upon whom God had heaped favours. Then,
having given the matter more thought she said, in a very
Thérèsian style, that she was only 'a very little saint'. Plainly she
worried about her own humility, whether she was genuinely
'humble of heart'. In the weakness and confinement of the

sickroom with her sisters' shining conviction about her continually voiced, or at least assumed, it was difficult to keep a sense of perspective.

Once, having implied to her sisters that they were looking after a saint she added 'But you are saints too!' It was as if the potentiality for sainthood was what mattered, not the human failure. She resisted, with some courage, both the affectations and the coynesses that Pauline encouraged. She refused to scatter rose petals to a group of the nuns who came to see her – that belonged to a different part of her life altogether, the intimate love she felt for Jesus. When Pauline saw her in the garden gazing at the sky she commented archly with what love she was looking towards heaven. Not at all, Thérèse said tartly. She was not thinking about the real heaven at all, a mystery that, in any case, seemed entirely closed to her, she was simply admiring the material world.

Maybe it was the cloying adulation of her relatives that made Mother Marie's naturally sardonic nature a welcome relief. In her critical eyes at least, the expectations were not high.

This attitude of Mother's chimed with Thérèse's present desire to taste humiliation 'to the brim'. It seemed to her that she needed to renounce 'the last shred of dignity', to feel like everyone's drudge, everyone's slave. Perhaps this was the genius of the 'Little Way'. To lie dying an excruciating death that took away the little privacies and forms of self-control which are precious to most of us, to endure almost unremitting pain, to have to rely upon others for the smallest services, to be an object of (not always kind) gossip in the convent, to be harried and cross-questioned by those who loved her most but who did not grant her peace, was to have 'the last shred of dignity' forcibly ripped away. What else to do then but to 'choose' it, to respond to it out of freedom rather than necessity?

Looking back over her life as a nun in that last summer she had written, interestingly, of the 'tangled undergrowth of Carmel'. Her intense idealisation of the life as an adolescent girl has given way to her mature understanding of the way good and bad are mixed up in the life there as they are everywhere else.

Humour appears now in her writing, small *aperçus* of convent conversations and conduct, full of irony.

A haymaking nun has just taken leave of me with the words: 'Poor little Sister, it must be very tiring for you to be writing like that all day.' 'Don't worry about that,' I said, 'I look as if I were writing a great deal, but there's hardly anything to show for it.' She seemed relieved at that. 'A good thing too,' she said, 'but all the same it's just as well we're getting the hay in; a bit of distraction for you.' I should think it did distract me, quite apart from the infirmarians' visits; it was no exaggeration to say that I hardly got anything written.[58]

This is Thérèse's form of grumbling.

Spending most of her days and nights in bed she pondered deeply about questions that had always interested her. She thinks about acts of charity, how it is easy to do them to create an impression or not to annoy somebody who has asked for help, and how the only kind of love that is really any good is the sort that is a free gift of oneself. Yet the more she thinks about it the more mysterious it all becomes and she feels that instead of writing any more she would like to 'throw away my pen'.

An interesting form of indignation emerges in these last writings of Thérèse, a sense of outrage that she has tried to swallow down and will now ignore no longer. Tiny vignettes of convent life suddenly emerge. 'I tell one of the Sisters, when we have leave to talk, about some light that has been given to me in prayer; and she, quite soon afterwards, mentions it to a third party in conversation as if it were an idea of her own; isn't that pilfering? Or again, in recreation, I whisper some remark to the person next to me, a good remark, absolutely to the point; and she repeats it aloud without mentioning where it came from; isn't that a theft of my property?' We hear the voice of a new Thérèse, the hint of the maturity of which tuberculosis robbed the Church. 'I can't say so at the time, but I'd like to; and if opportunity arises, I determine to let it be known, with all the delicacy in the world, that somebody's been misappropriating my thoughts.'[59]

A new, tougher Thérèse, with a clear mind of her own, peeps

out of this utterance, not so much little flower, as a powerful young tree. Yet she still has doubts – why should not her thoughts belong to others, is it pride that fuels her? And envy? She knows she has sometimes feared that Jesus loves others more than he loves her. She struggles on.

She remembers how, little prig that she was, in her early days at Carmel she had longed to set others right and tell them about faults in their behaviour. Nowadays she found herself thinking 'Thank goodness it isn't my job to put her right!' She ponders upon how it is the touchiest, silliest, most ignorant and irritating of the Sisters who need to be spoiled and loved by others, whereas it is always tempting to stick with the nicest and most balanced people. The only way to bear with the difficult ones is to see it as an act of love offered to Jesus.

As death comes nearer Thérèse ponders upon the lines in the Song of Songs 'Draw me after thee; we hasten' believing as she does that death is to be her union with her lover, Jesus. Only the suffering of getting to heaven is very great, is often unendurable to her.

The last six weeks of life were a series of crises. On 30 July they gave her the last rites and the whole community assembled in her room. She recovered but was in acute discomfort in any position she attempted to lie in as well as racked by pain in her intestines. She cried out 'Oh my God, oh my God, I can do no more, have mercy on me, have mercy on me.' The pain continued and Mother Marie continued opposed to the use of the hypodermic needle. 'What is the good of writing beautiful things about suffering?' Thérèse asked in bitterness. 'It means nothing, nothing! When you are going through it, then you know the worthlessness of all this eloquence.'

Receiving Communion had always been amongst the most precious experiences for Thérèse, but after the middle of August when she was continually vomiting blood she felt unable to take the sacrament. Her darkness was now almost total. She indicated to Pauline a well of shadow under the chestnut trees, and said that in such shadow she herself lay, body and soul. Her prayers to the saints fell, it seemed to her, upon deaf ears.

In extremis she took some comfort from lying with her arms extended as if on a crucifix.

On 29 September when the Prioress came to see her Thérèse asked her in a childlike way if this were the final agony and if so, what to do next. 'How does one die?' After another terrible night she rallied briefly and tried to face that she might go on living for months, in acute suffering. She held her crucifix and looked at it continually, often reiterating that she would suffer for as long as God wanted her to.

In the afternoon the end seemed near and the nuns assembled, but after two hours were sent away again. 'Am I not to die yet?' Thérèse asked. 'Very well, let it be so. I do not wish to suffer less.'

At seven in the evening the nuns were again summoned. Gazing at her crucifix Thérèse said, 'Oh, I love him. My God, I love you.' And died. The photograph of her taken after death shows a face beautiful, young, and peaceful.

Chapter Nine

THE SHOWER OF ROSES

'I will spend my Heaven in doing good upon earth,' Thérèse had said and when she was buried in the cemetery at Lisieux at a funeral attended only by Léonie and the Guérins, her sisters persuaded the Prioress to have these words inscribed on the cross on Thérèse's grave, in marked contrast to the plain graves of other nuns. In the weeks and months during which Thérèse had endured the long agony of her dying her three sisters had spoken in front of her and behind her back of the possibility that she was a saint. Now that she was dead there was work to be done in letting the world know of her spiritual achievement.

Her life, though exemplary and remarkable in many ways lacked one essential ingredient for official sanctity – miracles. Since these had not come in her lifetime then, if she was to pass, as it were, the canonisation examination, there must be miracles after death. There was certainly an atmosphere of the supernatural at Carmel in the days succeeding her death – rumours of unexplained perfume in the air, and a nun who had placed her head upon Thérèse's feet after death being cured of chronic headache, but this, although reassuring to the three Martin sisters and their cousin, was scarcely enough to startle the world. Thérèse had said that after her death she would let fall showers of rose petals. Whether she meant this as a reassuring sign to her sisters that she really had gone to heaven, whether she meant it in some metaphorical sense (i.e. the 'doing good on earth'), or whether it was even a sort of joke referring to her pleasure in flinging rose petals as a child in the Corpus Christi procession, is not at all clear. No rose petals appeared.

It was the custom, when a Carmelite died, to send round an obituary notice to other religious houses giving an account of the nun's life and maybe including a bit of her writing, if she was gifted in that way. The autobiographical writing of Thérèse seemed not only ideal for this purpose, but *so* good that it seemed a pity not to share it with a much wider audience. While Thérèse was still alive her sisters seem to have discussed this idea with her, and so keen was she, not exactly for the personal glory for which she had once longed, but for the chance that other 'little souls' might share her experience, that she had revelled in the idea. She knew that the writing, begun for her sisters, needed polishing if it was to be read by a wider audience. The first section, written out of her love for Pauline, was delightfully unselfconscious in its memories, a piece of work done for domestic pleasure and not for public consumption. The second section, addressed to Marie, and the third section, addressed to Mother Marie de Gonzague, are much more self-conscious and didactic, as if she has become aware of an audience there to be improved. The final pages must also have been affected by her acute physical weakness, her neat schoolgirl writing moving from ink to pencil, and finally into an unreadable scrawl. She entrusted Pauline with the task of doing whatever was necessary to make her little book or rather series of notebooks, fit for others to read.

What happened next suggested that not only the Martin sisters but also the Prioress and her spiritual advisers had begun to see, as it were, the untapped publicity potential of Thérèse. Pauline added some pious thoughts, cut some of the childhood reminiscences, and altered some details to make the portrait of the would-be saint more complete. Ida Görres suggests that, as Thérèse's first schoolmistress, Pauline quite naturally made corrections and 'improvements'. They somewhat lessened the vitality of Thérèse's style – Pauline, we may guess, would have written a much duller and more sentimental book. Maybe it was Pauline who suggested that the book should have the title *A Canticle of Love, or the Passing of an Angel*, a fancy which an interested cleric fortunately toned down to *The Story of a Soul*.

Work done on the text of *The Story of a Soul* in recent years suggests that some of the more florid literary forms apparently employed by Thérèse – the rhetorical questions, the philosophical ponderings – were Pauline's attempts to make her little sister's homely writing more 'literary'.

An imprimatur was needed from Thérèse's old adversary and friend, Monsignor Hugonin, the Bishop of Bayeux. He could not make up his mind to give this at first, claiming insultingly to be fearful of 'the imagination of women', but eventually did so (within a few weeks of his own death as it turned out), and just over a year after Thérèse's death the convent had two thousand copies printed, an extraordinary number, almost as if the nuns were publishing a novel. And just as if Thérèse was a novelist the book sold amazingly well – five thousand copies within the first two years; not the book alone, but also photographs of Thérèse, often with tiny pieces of her clothing or bed-linen, or wood from the furniture of her cell attached. Carmel had acquired a sort of ghoulish cottage industry for itself.

Not all the nuns liked or approved of this. Some of them did not think Thérèse deserved it, and some thought it was a scheme thought up for the glorification of the Martin sisters. Even the Martin sisters were not happy. Mother Marie de Gonzague had undertaken some final editing of her own when the manuscript left Pauline's hands, altering it so that it seemed as if all three of the texts had been addressed to her instead of only the last of them. She claimed that she had done it to make the book into a literary unity, but Pauline and Marie were very naturally furious. There was nothing they could do about it.

Possibly Thérèse's death and the stream of events which followed it had one other effect on the Martin relatives. Léonie, who must have been deeply ambivalent about religious life, since she had made three abortive attempts at it (once in the Poor Clares and twice in the Order of the Visitation), finally returned in 1899 to the convent of the Visitation and this time stayed there. The sister of a saint could not be found wanting in persistence.

The book had one immediate and striking effect which was

the stream of postulants wanting to enter the Lisieux Carmel. It is interesting to compare this with the flood of novice monks who wanted to enter the monastery of Gethsemani in Kentucky when Thomas Merton wrote a moving book about his experiences there in the 1940s. (It is also interesting to note similarities between Merton's autobiographical style and Thérèse's; he admitted to having a 'devotion' to her, and certain phrases he uses, and even more a sort of wry joking about the hardships of the life are extraordinarily reminiscent.)

Within a couple of years of Thérèse's death her fame was already growing fast. The first edition of *The Story of a Soul* having sold out by 1899, a second edition of four thousand copies was prepared and this too began to sell very quickly. The book was read first by religious and would-be religious, and gradually reached the Catholic public. They liked the sweetness and perhaps the sentimentality, they enjoyed Thérèse's capacity to tell a good story, they were moved, as we may still be moved today, by the sadness of her death at such an early age. Mortal illness, particularly from tuberculosis, was part of people's lives then in a way it is not part of ours, and everyone must have reflected and fantasised about such a death.

In the same way as the book had brought new postulants to Carmel it brought a flood of pilgrims to the cemetery in Lisieux, with renewed requests for pieces of clothing and other relics of Thérèse.

In 1902, too late to correct the final editing of *The Story of a Soul* Pauline was re-elected Prioress, a job which she held with only a brief respite until her death in 1923. During the months of Thérèse's dying she had filled a notebook with her sister's sayings. Over the years she worked at these, finally publishing them as a book – *Novissima Verba* – in 1927. Mother Marie de Gonzague died in 1904, her long struggle with the Martin sisters over at last. Tragically, cousin Marie Guérin, Sister Marie of the Eucharist, died in 1905 in the same painful way as Thérèse.

By 1906 the cult of Thérèse was far advanced. Many thousands of people had read her book, hundreds had prayed at her tomb and treasured pictures of her. Carmel, it was rumoured, was putting forward her case in Rome as a possible candidate for canonisation.

French missionaries had a particular liking for her – 'la petite soeur de France' as they called her. According to Ida Görres they mentioned her so frequently in Africa that the king of one tribe appointed her as 'Regent'. Our Lady herself took second place to her. In Portugal bishops granted indulgences to readers of *The Story of a Soul*, a practice which increased the book's popularity. In England there were requests to the Archbishop of Westminster to grant similar indulgences, but the Archbishop refused with a reply which cast some slight doubt on the integrity of Thérèse's relatives.

One of the fascinations of the story of Thérèse is that it reveals something of the social and psychological process by which a person is transformed into a saint. There is something essentially mysterious about the way in which any life – that of an actor, a writer, a pop star, a 'sex goddess' – breaks out of obscurity and becomes known to thousands, while others who lead similar lives remain largely unknown. Other women led good, pious lives, much like Thérèse's, in and out of convents, others died tragically in youth of the same dreadful disease. Others scribbled their thoughts in exercise books.

To touch public imagination in the way Thérèse did suggests a hunger, a longing, in the unconscious of hundreds of people. When they see pictures or hear a story of this particular young woman then immediately the experience locks into fantasies they scarcely knew they had, fantasies which carry great hope and longing. Thérèse, in her youth and sheltered existence, has the charm of innocence, of goodness, and perhaps of a sort of mediocrity. She is a sort of eternal schoolgirl. Her niceness and relative simplicity – the unspectacular simplicity of a young girl at home for the most part – is pleasant to read about. It is understandable that during the First World War many French soldiers went into battle carrying pictures and medals of her, and French airmen named an aeroplane after her. Not only might they have hoped for her supernatural intervention in the likely event of their deaths, but in the misery and squalor of the

trenches she offered a sort of promise that life might hold more
than the hell on earth of the fields of Flanders. If, on brief spells
from duty, they went in search of a different kind of woman who
held out a different kind of promise, this does not make the
Thérèse image any less bright – if anything it sharpens and
defines it.

Thérèse's death, though by no means an uncommon one in
her period, was dramatic, and nineteenth-century readers dearly
loved a good death-bed. In fact death-beds evoke fantasies in
most of us, fantasies of pathos, heroism, and of having our
lightest word raptly listened to. Sanctity and death carry a
tremendous imaginative appeal, the appeal of what it might be
like to become the idealised self within us, nobly shedding
our greedier and more egocentric traits in exchange for a life of
austerity or devotion to the poor.

Convents and monasteries, with their ordered lives, their
simplicity, poverty and chastity, their prayers and penances,
similarly encourage fantasies, as well as fascination at what life
in them must be like. Ignorance of it encourages all sorts of
projections upon the inhabitants, including the projection that
they must be infinitely better than the rest of us. If we cannot be
saints ourselves then we are interested in those who live that
unlived part of our lives for us. Thérèse, who retired from the
world so early, who lived out incredible austerities, who suffered
a long and painful death with heroism, and who had her dying
speeches carefully recorded by her sisters, was in all these ways a
good candidate for spiritual popularity.

Like the saints of the early Church her fame spread through
rumour until she was so popular that the Church had to take
official notice of her. A fillip was given to the movement which
wanted to declare Thérèse a saint by an impressive miracle. In
1906 a young seminarian called Abbé Anne was in the final
stages of pulmonary tuberculosis. A novena was said to Thérèse,
but without success, and the Abbé's relatives awaited his
immediate death. The young man pressed a relic of Thérèse to
his heart and begged her to cure him. Instantly he was well.
'The destroyed and ravaged lungs had been replaced by new

lungs, carrying out their normal functions and about to revive the entire organism. A slight emaciation persists, which will disappear within a few days under a regularly assimilated diet,' wrote a contemporary doctor.

Here was one major and well-attested miracle to be ascribed to Thérèse. There were to be many more. Not surprisingly recoveries from tuberculosis were high on the list of miracles ascribed to Thérèse, but her name was evoked for every sort of ailment, not least for driving out devils in exorcism ceremonies. Blindness, deformity, human distress of every kind, was healed by the 'little saint', a stream of cures which represented the 'shower of roses' she had once promised.

Meanwhile the 'machinery' of the Church had gone into gear. In 1907 the Bishop of Bayeux had ordered the Lisieux Carmel to hand over its souvenirs of Thérèse, presumably on the grounds that they might be potential relics. In 1909 a Pleader and Vice-Pleader were appointed by Rome (in Rome and France respectively) to prepare the 'Cause' of Thérèse. In August 1910 a 'Process' began to examine her writings, and in September her body was exhumed from the Lisieux cemetery. Aware that Thérèse was, in a sense, 'on trial', the faithful began writing in their hundreds to attest to her holiness – in a year Carmel had received nearly ten thousand letters of this kind. The rain of letters was to grow until in one day in 1918 five hundred and twelve letters would be received. The dossier on her in Rome ran to thousands of words, and necessitated many hours of committees.

In 1914 Rome officially approved of the writings of Thérèse and Pius X signed the document which served as the introduction of the 'Cause'. Privately he had declared that he believed Thérèse to be the greatest saint of modern times.

In spite of this, the Church was slower and more reluctant than public opinion. Supremely in France, but throughout Europe, in South America, French Canada, the United States, Africa and China, Thérèse was invoked. Even Protestants took to her.

In 1921 a decree was promulgated by Pope Benedict XV by

which Thérèse became 'Venerable', as odd an adjective for the 24-year-old nun as it had seemed for Joan of Arc. 'This maiden, so modest, so humble, this child' as the Pope described her. In 1923 Pope Pius XI promulgated the decree which beatified Thérèse, describing her as 'the star of his pontifical reign'. Determined that Thérèse should attain the final accolade of canonisation, eight hundred to a thousand correspondents a day wrote to Carmel.

Finally, on 17 May 1925, Thérèse Martin, Soeur Thérèse de l'Enfant-Jésus et de la Sainte Face was canonised at St Peter's in the presence of thirty-four cardinals, more than two hundred archbishops and bishops, and innumerable priests, religious and others. The basilica was decorated with garlands of roses. It was packed – it was thought there were about sixty thousand people in the congregation, and the square outside was jammed with pilgrims. Mass was said and the banner of the new saint was carried down the aisle. A few rose petals fell mysteriously from the ceiling during the course of the ceremonies. It was 'gloire' beyond anything the child Thérèse could have imagined.

Conclusion

For years after her death Thérèse played an important part in the Catholic imagination, particularly in France and more particularly in Normandy. Many churches and cathedrals erected statues to her, wearing her Carmelite habit and clutching the white roses which were her hallmark. Village churches in France still display the touching little plaques with which the sick thanked her for prayers answered and for recovery from illness. An opulent basilica was built in Lisieux in honour of Thérèse, inaugurated in 1937 by Cardinal Pacelli, later Pope Pius XII, a huge building for a small town which already has a large cathedral and many churches. Here pilgrims come in coachloads to see the relics of Thérèse, and the graves of Louis and Zélie, who were reburied on the site. There are films about Thérèse on display, souvenirs and books to be bought. On the other side of the town Les Buissonets has its trail of visitors, as does the little house in Alençon where Thérèse was born.

There have been innumerable books about Thérèse, the majority of them written by priests, for whom she seems to have a particular appeal. Certainly the most fulsome biographies of her have been written by men, many of whom emphasise her painful obedience, her penitential life, her submissiveness, her dutifulness – erstwhile womanly qualities that do not make an immediate appeal to twentieth-century taste.

Thérèse was, of course, brought up to know woman's place, which was either in the home, often in childbed, or in the convent. As a good nun she naturally practised obedience (excessively, the modern reader may feel, since she wrecked her health in the process). Yet in spite of this she feels a quirkier and more subversive character than many of her priest-admirers manage to suggest, whether arguing with the Pope at a papal audience when she was only fourteen (something few other papal callers of any age have had the nerve to attempt), or making astringent comments on her death-bed when those who ministered to her – her sisters, the doctor, the chaplain – seemed not fully to understand her point of view. So firmly is this side of her character ignored that it is possible to feel that what appeals to many in Thérèse, is that she can be moulded in fantasy to an image many priests have preferred for women – sexless, obedient, gentle and good – the model of 'safety'.

She can, of course, easily be presented in this light, and her depression and invalidism seem the lot of those who are 'too good'. Yet alongside the rigidities of her class, time and calling, there is something strong, original and irrepressible in Thérèse which I wonder if some of her male adulators recognise and appreciate as eagerly as they appreciate her dutiful qualities – a toughness, a sharpness, a splendidly incurable independence of mind which transcended her meagre education, and which even in sickness and mortal agony did not desert her.

She might be seen, paradoxically, as a model for the power, endurance, and resourcefulness of women, a power which, even when intolerably constricted, crushed and punished by circumstances, reasserts itself with the tenacity of a weed (or little flower) growing on a wall. She is naive, impoverished both by her lack of learning and by her inadequate experience of life outside the convent walls, but neither she nor her superiors succeeded in concealing her untutored intelligence and her native shrewdness. She had one other worldly asset; spoiled child as she was, she had a natural taste for getting her own way without even noticing that this was what she was doing.

What are *we*, a hundred years on, with a different reading of human psychology from the nineteenth century, to make of the life of Thérèse? Even if we share the same religious faith as the saint we have some unease about the traditional interpretations of her life, as, it must be said, did many irreproachable Catholics who were her contemporaries. They were mainly troubled by the sentimentality, and a few of them attributed that to Thérèse's infantility, symbolised by her oft-repeated use of the word 'little', mainly for herself who was not little in any sense of the word. They sensed a spurious humility in it.

Our criticism might have more to do with a sense of being taken in, of a feeling that her sanctity is somehow a trick that has been brought off by the Martin sisters with some collusion from Thérèse. This is not necessarily to accuse the sisters of malice – they had been brought up in an atmosphere in which sanctity was the only imaginable good – yet any careful examination of the facts makes it clear that for what seemed to them an excellent end they were prepared to behave in manipulative ways, towards the convent, the Church, and not least their dying sister.

We may feel that the entire Martin family were the victims of a rigid bourgeois society, complacent in its provincialism, narrow in its culture, restricted in its religious understanding. Louis and Zélie, themselves disappointed in religious vocations, pushed their daughters as inevitably towards the convent as Mrs Worthington pushed her daughter towards the stage. The suffering of Léonie, joining and leaving convents three times before her final submission, would seem to indicate something of the pressure involved. Marie had felt no burning sense of vocation either, yet inevitably she too was confined in the silence and austerity of Carmel. If in doubt, seemed to be the Martin family motto, then you cannot do better than take the veil.

Zélie, a woman of iron will and strict discipline, undoubtedly set the religious tone of the family, a tone that was maintained, despite her early death, by Pauline, in many ways a kind of double for her mother. Marie, a more balanced personality, and Céline, a fairly phlegmatic and unimaginative one, struck a more moderate note. Léonie, always 'different' and unable to conform to her mother's ideas, alone put up a sort of fight, an unequal struggle which condemned her to bitter suffering. Thérèse, as the last and most delicate child, and the one with most imagination and intelligence, also suffered – it was not possible for her to live out the smallest rebellion from a way of life that had been chosen for her in the cradle.

The shock of renewed separations from the first weeks of her life, and the rigidity of Zélie's discipline, gave her a lasting terror of abandonment and of not measuring up to the standards expected of her. Even before Zélie's death, and Pauline's rigorous application of her mother's ideas, Thérèse was a profoundly insecure child tormented with the fear of 'not being good', or of 'not pleasing God', racked with scruples, unable to relate successfully with her peers, somehow stuck in the 'little queen' role assigned to her by her father, one not calculated to appeal to other children. Louis's obvious passion for her in which her lightest word could please or distress him robbed her of the strong, balanced support which might have gone some little way to dissolving her fears. Uncle Isidore came near to filling the role of a father and brings an air of commonsense into the story whenever he is mentioned.

In addition to the particular problem of being Thérèse Martin of Alençon and Lisieux was the more general problem of being a woman in the nineteenth century. Zélie had illustrated the physical strain of perpetual childbearing, the sadness of losing three children to 'heaven' and of an illness, possibily accentuated by childbearing, which killed her at forty-five. Perhaps because of the underlying incestuousness of the relationship with Louis Thérèse does not seem to have been drawn to men except as father figures – any suggestion of sexuality is ruthlessly repressed. So marriage, for these various reasons, could not have appealed to her.

The religious life, the frustrated ambition of her parents, very clearly did. That she found it congenial to her temperament is not in question. But much that emerges in her writings and sayings makes it clear that its relative passivity disappointed a whole side of her character which would love to have been a travelling missionary, a hero, a soldier, above all a priest. To be a woman was to be condemned to confinement, the rule of others, the lack of a voice with which to make oneself heard, and the absence of an attentive audience to listen.

Thérèse was self-confessedly ambitious and she suffered,

therefore, from obscurity, the lack of opportunity to go out and make an active impact on the world, even though her upbringing had made the world seem a dangerous and wicked place from which it was safer and wiser to retreat.

Energies denied their natural expression turn inward. Like many women before her Thérèse made a virtue of the suffering she endured, telling herself that this was what Jesus had chosen for her, though it might seem to others that it was not Jesus but a particular social and religious framework that condemned her to it. In a life that was a sort of death-in-life she was unashamedly enthusiastic for death (as she had been since the age of three), in itself the sign, we may think, of a deep despair. We cannot know how much a longing for death influences the processes of the body, making it vulnerable to disease, but Thérèse, at least, was not in the least surprised or outraged to realise, at the age of twenty-three, that death was already very near. Neither the living conditions of Carmel, nor its attitude to death, made it possible or desirable to put up a fight for life. On the contrary, with its curious mixture of denial of facts, stubbornness and masochism, it pushed Thérèse towards her fate.

Though it aspired to great religious heights, the human reality of the Lisieux Carmel was, by all accounts, a depressing one. The brides of Christ, as depicted not least in Thérèse's own writing, were petty, envious, jealous and downright unkind. Mother Marie de Gonzague may have been seriously unbalanced – indeed that is the kindest diagnosis one can make of a 'Mother' who appears to have 'played off' her daughters' affections one against another, who allowed one of them to struggle on with duties far beyond her strength to the point of irredeemable physical breakdown, and who refused the relief of morphia to a dying patient in intolerable agony. It is a form of Christianity so perverse as to be quite intolerable.

The truly remarkable thing about Thérèse, however, is that she took her own very human failings – her longing for love and attention and acclaim, her overweening spiritual ambition – exactly as they were in all their silliness and childishness, and began to work with them. Almost as if she were considering

another person, not herself, she detached herself from the particular shame of such feelings by the process of owning them.
Cruelly debarred by the accidents of her upbringing and the
blindness of Church and society from leading the rich life her
body and brains might have enjoyed, she took the scrap of life
allowed to her and transformed it.

It is easy to underestimate how considerable her achievement
was, simply because we may resent her collusion with a Church
which oppressed women. In a period in which women have
begun to claim their birthrights we may resent the acquiescence
of Christian women in forms of life which suppressed, silenced
and destroyed them. Yet pity and understanding of their plight
helps us to interpret the kind of battle they were surreptitiously
waging. Thérèse chose to acquiesce because she could not have
imagined any other choice, but then she did something daring
and interesting with her acquiescence. She was, she knew in-
distinctly, one of a great army of human beings (the 'little'),
whom life had robbed of much that might have been theirs.
Very well then, she would celebrate the feast of those who have
nothing, who have not lived. The Little Way, far from being the
tool of subservience (especially for women) that it has often been
made into, has an almost ironic quality to it. 'If I may have
nothing,' it says gaily, 'then I will turn reason inside out and
make having nothing the most enjoyable of possibilities.' Like a
St Francis, like a hero of a Solzhenitsyn novel who discovers that
when everything has been taken from a man and he no longer
has anything to lose then he is free, so Thérèse, on behalf of
womankind, charts a way to live out an impossible situation. She
also reveals the price that is paid in the attempt to make a true
rather than a false response to life.

In a bizarre way, a way that echoes the subversion of the
gospels themselves, she triumphs. Paradoxically the voiceless
nun finds a voice that is heard more resoundingly than that of
any priest or even Pope, of her generation. Humble, insignifi-
cant, 'little', she intends to find an audience and she does.

What is it she has to say, though? She speaks for those driven,
forced, by the cruel necessity of social constraint, religious

taboo, accident, physical or mental handicap and disability, into a life they would never have chosen if they had been more fortunate. Cripplingly shy, hysterical, totally ensnared by her family in the net of 'love', debarred by social convention from pouring out her formidable energies in the world, Thérèse turns inward, becomes an invalid (like so many women of her generation) and begins to till the dreary acres of 'submission'. If there is no choice in life, no way out of the trap, then only one response is left; the religious trick is to turn it from masochism into love. Anger gives way not merely to acceptance but to a strange sort of play-acting that gradually turns into the truth – a play-acting that says this is the best of all possible happenings, that this bout of pain is the purest piece of luck. In other words that it is the will of God. By such an act of surrender the unbearable pain of crucifixion is transmuted into the joy of resurrection. The far side of the coin, the opposite side from the face of pain, is the face of joy. 'Love', as e.e. cummings says, 'makes the little thickness of the coin.'

Thérèse, handicapped in Church and society for being a woman, illustrates a favourite paradox of Jesus, that the stone that the builders rejected becomes the carved cornice, a matter of pride. Was she a saint? At the time of her canonisation Cardinal Vico pointed out how in the early days of the Church people became saints by popular acclaim. Nobody collected careful bits of evidence about them. They were those who, for largely inexplicable reasons, became popular among the faithful as somehow illustrating what the faith meant to them. Some performed miracles, some preached marvellously, some lived lives of loneliness in the desert, some were wonderful at hearing confessions and giving advice, some did nothing much except give others a feeling of joy and hope, in bad times as in good. A saint was not somebody who had been put through the Vatican mangle, but was simply a focus of love.

Not for several centuries had there been a popular saint in the sense Thérèse became one, one from whom ordinary people drew encouragement and whom they received as their own.

BIBLIOGRAPHY

Autobiography

Sainte Thérèse de l'Enfant-Jésus et de la Sainte Face, *Histoire d'une Ame*, Les Editions du Cerf, Paris, 1985

Thérèse of Lisieux, *Autobiography of a Saint: The story of a soul*, trans. by Ronald Knox, Fontana, London, 1960

Books about Thérèse of Lisieux

V. Sackville-West, *The Eagle and the Dove*, Michael Joseph, London, 1943

Hans Urs von Balthasar, *Thérèse of Lisieux*, Sheed and Ward, London, 1953

Etienne Robo, *Two portraits of St Teresa of Lisieux*, Sands & Co., London, 1955

Ida Friederike Görres, *The Hidden Face – a study of St Thérèse of Lisieux*, Burns & Oates, Tunbridge Wells, 1959

Jean-François Six, *La Véritable Enfance de Thérèse de Lisieux*, Editions du Seuil, Paris, 1971

Michael Hollings, *Thérèse of Lisieux*, William Collins Sons & Co., 1981, Fount Paperbacks, London, 1982

Eric Doyle, 'The Ordination of Women in the Roman Catholic Church' (essay), *Feminine in the Church* ed. Monica Furlong, SPCK, London, 1984

Background material

Teresa of Avila, *The Life of Saint Teresa* (of Avila), Penguin Classics, London, 1957

Rodolphe Hoornaert, *Saint Teresa* (of Avila) *in her writings*, Sheed and Ward, London, 1931

Thomas Merton, *The Seven Storey Mountain*, Harcourt, Brace & Company, New York, 1948

Anne Hardman, *English Carmelites in Penal Times*, Burns Oates & Washbourne, London, 1936

Rudolph M. Bell and David Weinstein, *Saints and Society*, University of Chicago Press, Chicago, 1982

Rudolph M. Bell, *Holy Anorexia*, University of Chicago Press, Chicago, 1985

The Oxford Dictionary of the Christian Church, Oxford University Press, Oxford, 1977

The Oxford Dictionary of Saints, Oxford University Press, Oxford, 1978

Dictionary of Saints, Penguin, London, 1965

NOTES

CHAPTER 1: For Ever and Ever

1. Henri Pranzini was tried in July 1887 for murdering a woman, her maid and her eleven-year-old daughter in Paris by cutting their throats – his case aroused enormous interest in France. Although found guilty he refused to admit the crime or show remorse. Thérèse prayed earnestly for him after he was condemned to death, and believed that when he kissed the crucifix before being executed it was because of repentance due to her prayers.
2. Père Pichon: A Jesuit and gifted confessor who had helped Marie Martin with her guilty 'scruples'. He was much influenced by the French spiritual writers François de Sales (1567–1622) and Jean Pierre de Caussade (1675–1751) and preached a more loving and forgiving God than Zélie and Aunt Dosithée had taught the Martin children to expect.
3. Sainte Thérèse, *Histoire d'une Ame*, p. 174, Les Editions du Cerf, Paris, 1985.

CHAPTER 2: The Little Queen

4. Letter from Zélie to Céline Guérin, 2 January 1873.
5. Letter from Zélie to Pauline, 25 June 1874.
6. Letter from Zélie to Pauline, 21 May 1876.
7. Letter from Zélie to Pauline, 22 March 1877.
8. Letter from Zélie to Pauline, 4 March 1877.
9. Letter from Zélie to Céline Guérin, 17 December 1876.
10. Letter from Zélie to Pauline, 13 February 1877.
11. Letter from Zélie to Pauline, 21 May 1876.

12. Etienne Robo, *Two Portraits of St Teresa of Lisieux*, p. 178, Sands, London, 1955.
13. *Histoire d'une Ame*, Manuscript A, p. 31.
14. *Summarium* quoted by Ida Friederike Görres in *The Hidden Face*, p. 52, Burns & Oates, Tunbridge Wells, 1959.
15. *Histoire d'une Ame*, p. 54.
16. *Histoire d'une Ame*, p. 39.
17. Letter from Zélie to Pauline, spring 1877.

CHAPTER 3: Born for Greatness

18. *Histoire d'une Ame*, p. 43.
19. ibid., p. 51.
20. ibid., p. 53.
21. ibid., p. 53.
22. Ida Friederike Görres, p.59.
23. The Abbey school was a sixteenth-century Benedictine foundation, run by the Benedictine Abbey de Notre Dame du Pré in Lisieux. It was destroyed during the Second World War.
24. *Histoire d'une Ame*, p. 63.
25. ibid., p. 65.
26. ibid., p. 70.
27. ibid., p. 70.
28. ibid., p. 71.
29. ibid., p. 72.
30. ibid., p. 75.
31. ibid., p. 77.
32. ibid., pp. 78–79.

CHAPTER 4: A Drop Lost in the Ocean.

33. ibid., p. 91.
34. Thomas à Kempis (c. 1380–1471), *The Imitation of Christ*: An ascetical writer who greatly influenced Thérèse.
35. *Histoire d'une Ame*, p. 97.
36. ibid., p. 103.
37. ibid., p. 104.
38. ibid., pp. 109, 110, 126.

CHAPTER 5: A Toy of No Value

41. ibid., p. 157.
42. ibid., p. 157.
43. ibid., p. 159.
44. ibid., p. 168.

CHAPTER 6: The Little Bride

45. ibid., pp. 179, 180.
46. ibid., p. 183.
47. ibid., p. 181.
48. Billet de Profession, ibid., p. 315.
49. ibid., p. 191.

CHAPTER 7: The Little Way

50. ibid., p. 200.
51. ibid., Manuscript B, p. 220.
52. ibid., p. 221.
53. ibid., Manuscript C, p. 273.
54. Etienne Robo, pp. 152 ff.
55. Quoted by Etienne Robo, source not given.
56. *Histoire d'une Ame*, p. 234.
57. ibid., pp. 245, 246.
58. ibid., p. 285.
59. ibid., p. 262.

INDEX

Adam and Eve, 2
Africa, 125, 127
Agnes, Sister *see* Martin, Pauline
Alençon, 6, 24, 25, 27, 38, 52–3,
    59–60, 99, 129
Anne, Abbé, 126–7
Anne of Jesus, Mother, 102
Aquinas, St Thomas, 3
Assisi, 71
Association of the Holy Angels, 58
Augustine, Saint, 3
Autobiography of a Saint, 1, 44–5,
    78, 84, 99–100, 108–11, 117–
    19, 122–4, 125
Avila, 75

Bayeux, 66
Benedict, St, 74
Benedict XV, Pope, 127–8
Benedictine Order, 74
Berthold, St, 74
Bologna, 69
Bonaventure, 4
Brontë family, 103
Les Buissonets, Lisieux, 11–13, 15,
    38–9, 46, 93, 108, 129
Bunyan, John, 113

Caen, 64, 87
Calvinism, 6, 8
Canada, 127
Carmel, Pauline enters, 47–9;
    Thérèse determines to become a
    nun at, 47–8, 62–3, 64–8,

70–3; and Thérèse's vision of the
    Virgin, 51; Marie joins, 59, 60;
    Thérèse enters, 8, 11–23;
    Thérèse's life as a nun at 78–88,
    92–3; and Thérèse's
    autobiography, 123–4; and the
    canonisation of Thérèse, 127
Carmelite Order, 74-7
Cecilia, St, 70
celibacy, 3–4
Chalet des Lilas, Trouville, 58
The Children of Mary, 58
China, 127
Christianity, attitudes to women,
    2–5
Church Fathers, 3
Church of Our Lady of Victories,
    Paris, 50
Convent of the Visitation, Caen, 64
Convent of the Visitation, Le Mans,
    13, 24, 33–4
convents, 4–6
Cornières, Dr de, 114
Counter Reformation, 75

Delatroette, Canon, 14–15
Discalced Carmelites, 76
Domin, Abbé, 54
Dosithée, Sister *see* Guérin, Elise
dualism, 2–3
Ducellier, M., 41

England, 125
Enlightenment, 6

First World War, 125–6
Florence, 71–2
Francis of Assisi, St, 4, 134

Geneviève, Mother, 83, 85, 88, 89–90, 91
Genoa, 71
Gethsemani, monastery of, 124
Gonzague, Mother Marie de, 77, 98; and Thérèse's determination to become a nun, 47–8, 14–15, 72; relations with Thérèse, 18, 22, 80–5, 101–2, 105, 109–11; loses position of Reverend Mother, 93–4; becomes Mistress of Novices, 97; and Thérèse's memoirs, 100, 108–11, 123; and Thérèse's illness, 101–2, 103–5, 106–7, 113–14, 117, 119; mental instability, 133; death, 124
Görres, Ida, 40, 43, 122, 125
Great St Bernard monastery, 25
Greece, 2
Guérin, Céline, 12, 38–9, 49, 58, 65, 121
Guérin, Elise (Sister Dosithée), 24, 33–4
Guérin, Isidore (Thérèse's uncle), 6, 14, 24, 42, 58, 121; disapproves of Thérèse's decision to become a nun, 12, 23, 64–5; and Zélie's death, 36–7; Martin family stays with, 38–9; friendship with Thérèse, 49, 50, 132
Guérin, Jeanne, 12, 38–9, 91, 113
Guérin, Marie (Sister Marie of the Eucharist), 12, 38–9, 46, 48, 59, 107, 124

Hugonin, Monsignor, Bishop of Bayeux, 65–8, 72, 87, 91, 123, 127

Italy, 69

Jansen, Cornelius, 6
Jansenism, 6–7
Jesus Christ, 2, 21, 22, 57, 65, 71, 72, 82, 87, 89–90, 94–6, 107, 111, 119, 133, 135
Joan of Arc, 39, 95, 98, 116, 128
John of the Cross, St, 15
Joseph, St, 26, 52
Judaism, 2

Kempis, Thomas à, *Imitation of Christ*, 56, 61–2, 63
Knox, Ronald, 1

Le Mans, 24, 33
Leo XIII, Pope, 70–1
Le Lexovien, 6
Lisieux, 6, 7, 38–9, 99, 129
'Little Way', 7, 96–7, 102, 117, 134
Louise (maid), 34, 36, 38
Lourdes, 36

Madeleine, Sister, 92
Manes, 2–3
Manicheism, 2–3
Marie of the Angels, Sister (Novice Mistress), 14–15, 16, 19–21, 80
Marie of the Eucharist, Sister *see* Guérin, Marie
Marie of the Sacred Heart, Sister *see* Martin, Marie
Marie of the Trinity, Sister, 105
Martin, Céline (Thérèse's sister), 8, 17, 20, 61, 64, 72; childhood, 11, 26, 28, 33, 34–6; and Thérèse's determination to become a nun, 12–13, 19, 62, friendship with Thérèse, 31, 46–7, 62; and her mother's death, 38; education, 39, 45, 54; first communion, 47; and Thérèse's illness, 49; leaves school, 57; grand tour of Europe, 68–72; decides to become a nun, 87, 94; life as a nun, 98; nurses Thérèse, 106, 108, 114; and Thérèse's sanctity, 121, 131; death, 1

Martin, Léonie (Thérèse's sister), 11, 17, 20, 87, 121; childhood, 26, 28–9, 30, 34–5, 44; and her mother's death, 38; education, 39, 45; attempts to become a nun, 12–13, 60, 64, 123, 131; and Thérèse's illness, 49, 50; godmother to Thérèse, 57

Martin, Louis (Thérèse's father), 17, 91, 107; childhood, 25; marriage, 25–6; retirement, 26–7; relationship with Thérèse, 29, 31, 40–2, 57, 61, 132; spirituality, 32–3; and Zélie's death, 37, 38; and Thérèse's education, 45–6; and Thérèse's determination to become a nun, 62–3, 64–8; suffers a stroke, 62–3; grand tour of Europe, 68–72; and Thérèse's entry into Carmel, 11–14, 20–1, 86–7; mental illness, 86–8, 89; death, 87, 94, grave, 129

Martin, Marie (Sister Marie of the Sacred Heart, Thérèse's sister), 16, 49; birth, 26; and Thérèse's childhood, 27, 28, 32, 33; in the Convent of the Visitation, 33–4; runs Martin household, 36; and her mother's death, 38; and Thérèse's illness, 50, 106; and Thérèse's vision of the Virgin, 51; and Thérèse's First Communion, 53–4; becomes a nun, 13–14, 21, 59, 60, 86, 87, 131; and Thérèse's determination to become a nun, 17, 19, 62, 81–2; and Thérèse's memoirs, 99, 123; and Thérèse's sanctity, 114–17, 121, 131

Martin, Marie-Hélène, 26, 30–1

Martin, Marie-Joseph-Jean Baptiste, 26

Martin, Marie-Joseph-Louis, 26

Martin, Marie-Melanie-Thérèse, 26

Martin, Pauline (Sister Agnes, Thérèse's sister), 11, 16, 17, 70, 91; birth, 26; and Thérèse's childhood, 28, 32, 33; in the Convent of the Visitation, 33, 34; runs Martin household, 36; and her mother's death, 38; takes over role of Thérèse's mother, 39–44, 59; becomes a nun, 13, 47–8, 52, 56, 77; and Thérèse's First Communion, 53; and Thérèse's determination to become a nun, 14, 19, 22, 62, 72; relations with Thérèse as a nun, 80, 81–2; becomes Reverend Mother, 93–4, 97; and Thérèse's memoirs, 99, 100, 108, 122–3; and Thérèse's illness, 105, 106, 112; and Thérèse's sanctity, 114–17, 121, 131; re-elected Prioress, 124; publishes *Novissima Verba*, 124

Martin, Thérèse *see* Thérèse of Lisieux, St

Martin, Zélie (Thérèse's mother), 59, 65; letters, 7, 28, 29, 32; childhood, 24; lace-making business, 6, 24, 26–7; marriage, 25–6; children, 6, 26–7, 132; breast cancer, 6, 26, 34, 36–7; and Thérèse's childhood, 27–33; spirituality, 32–3, 131; death, 37, 38, 51, 93; grave, 129

Mary, Virgin, 4, 26; Thérèse sees vision of, 11, 50, 51–2

Mary Magdalen, St, 54

Maudelonde family, 46

Merton, Thomas, 124

Middle East, 2

Milan, 69

Naples, 71

Néele, Dr, 113–14

Le Normand, 6

Normandy, 6, 129

Novissima Verba, 124

Order of the Visitation, 123

Orwell, George, 105

Our Lady of Victories, Paris, 68

Oxford Dictionary of Saints, 9

Padua, 69
Palestine, 74
Papinau, Madame, 57
Paris, 25, 49, 68
Paul, St, 2, 8, 96
Peter, Mother, 86
Pichon, Père, 21, 91, 94
Pisa, 71
Pius X, Pope, 127
Pius XI, Pope, 128
Pius XII, Pope, 129
Pompeii, 71
Poor Clares, 13, 24, 60, 123
Port-Royal, 6
Portugal, 125
Pranzini, 15, 61, 77

Reformed Carmelites, 76
Reverony, M., 67, 68, 70–1
Robo, Etienne, 104
Rome, 68, 69–71, 127–8

Sackville-West, Vita, 1
Saint-Cyran, 6
St Peter's, Rome, 128
saints, 8–10
Semallé, 27
sexuality, Church's attitude to, 2–5
Sisters of St Vincent de Paul, 24
Solzhenitsyn, Alexander, 134
South America, 127
Spain, 75
The Story of a Soul, 1, 44–5, 78, 84,
    99–100, 108–11, 117–19, 122–
    4, 125
Strasbourg, 25
Switzerland, 68

Taillé, Rose, 27, 31
Teresa of Avila, St, 42, 75–7
Tertullian, 8
Thérèse of Lisieux, St, birth and
    separation from her mother, 27–
    8; childhood, 6, 27–37; early
    spirituality, 5, 21, 32, 35;
    relationship with her father, 29,
    31, 41–2, 57, 61, 132; character,
    30–2, 44–5; friendship with

Céline, 31, 46–7, 62; and her
    mother's death, 37, 51; Pauline
    brings up, 39–44, 59; education,
    39–40, 45–6, 54, 57–8; first
    confession, 41; visits Trouville,
    44, 58; and Pauline's decision to
    become a nun, 47–9, 52, 59;
    determination to become a nun,
    47–8, 52, 62–3, 64–8, 70–3;
    illnesses, 48–50, 57–8, 82;
    vision of the Virgin Mary, 50,
    51–2; visits Alençon, 52–3;
    First Communion, 53–4, 55–7;
    fascination with suffering, 56–7,
    95–6, 97; prays for Pranzini, 61,
    77; grand tour of Europe, 68–72;
    enters Carmel, 11–23; life as a
    nun, 78–88, 92–3, 97–8;
    relations with Reverend Mother,
    80–5, 101–2, 105, 109–11;
    received into Carmelite Order,
    86; profession, 88–91; vision of
    the devil, 89–90; poetry, 93;
    paintings, 93; fantasy life, 95–6;
    'Little Way', 7, 96–7, 102, 117,
    134; writes play about Joan of
    Arc, 98; tuberculosis, 101–5,
    106–8, 111–20; attitude to
    death, 107–8, 133;
    autobiography, 1, 78, 84, 99–
    100, 108–11, 117–19, 122–4,
    125; sanctity, 114–17, 121, 124–
    7, 131; relics, 115, 123, 124, 127,
    129; death, 120, 121, 126;
    miracles, 126–7; biographies,
    129; canonisation, 9, 127–8, 135;
    achievements, 133–5

Trouville, 44, 58

United States of America, 127

Venice, 69
Vico, Cardinal, 135
Victoire (maid), 12, 18, 41, 49, 99
Voltaire, 6

Westminster, Archbishop of, 125
women, Christian attitudes to, 2–5